31 Days Before Your CCNA Exam

Scott Bennett

Cisco Press ▪ 800 East 96th Street ▪ Indianapolis, Indiana 46240 USA

R 2007 08 24   Phase

31 Days Before Your CCNA Exam

Scott Bennett

Published by:
Cisco Press
800 East 96th Street
Indianapolis, IN 46240 USA

Printed in the United States of America 1 2 3 4 5 6 7 8 9 0

First Printing   August 2006

Library of Congress Cataloging-in-Publication Number: 2005938126

ISBN: 1-58713-174-9

Warning and Disclaimer

This book is designed to provide information about the Cisco Networking Academy Program CCNA curriculum. Every effort has been made to make this book as complete and as accurate as possible, but no warranty or fitness is implied.

The information is provided on an "as is" basis. The authors, Cisco Press, and Cisco Systems, Inc., shall have neither liability nor responsibility to any person or entity with respect to any loss or damages arising from the information contained in this book or from the use of the discs or programs that may accompany it.

The opinions expressed in this book belong to the author and are not necessarily those of Cisco Systems, Inc.

Feedback Information

At Cisco Press, our goal is to create in-depth technical books of the highest quality and value. Each book is crafted with care and precision, undergoing rigorous development that involves the unique expertise of members from the professional technical community.

Readers' feedback is a natural continuation of this process. If you have any comments regarding how we could improve the quality of this book, or otherwise alter it to better suit your needs, you can contact us through e-mail at feedback@ciscopress.com. Please make sure to include the book title and ISBN in your message.

We greatly appreciate your assistance.

Publisher	Paul Boger
Cisco Representative	Anthony Wolfenden
Cisco Press Program Manager	Jeff Brady
Executive Editor	Mary Beth Ray
Production Manager	Patrick Kanouse
Development Editor	Dayna Isley
Project Editor	Tonya Simpson
Copy Editor	Emily Rader
Technical Editors	Mark R. Anderson, Glenn Wright
Team Coordinator	Vanessa Evans
Book and Cover Designer	Louisa Adair
Composition	Bronkella Publishing LLC
Indexer	Heather McNeill

Trademark Acknowledgments

All terms mentioned in this book that are known to be trademarks or service marks have been appropriately capitalized. Cisco Press or Cisco Systems, Inc. cannot attest to the accuracy of this information. Use of a term in this book should not be regarded as affecting the validity of any trademark or service mark.

Corporate and Government Sales

Cisco Press offers excellent discounts on this book when ordered in quantity for bulk purchases or special sales.

For more information please contact: U.S. Corporate and Government Sales 1-800-382-3419 corpsales@pearsontechgroup.com

For sales outside the U.S. please contact: International Sales international@pearsoned.com

CISCO SYSTEMS

Corporate Headquarters	European Headquarters	Americas Headquarters	Asia Pacific Headquarters
Cisco Systems, Inc.	Cisco Systems International BV	Cisco Systems, Inc.	Cisco Systems, Inc.
170 West Tasman Drive	Haarlerbergpark	170 West Tasman Drive	Capital Tower
San Jose, CA 95134-1706	Haarlerbergweg 13-19	San Jose, CA 95134-1706	168 Robinson Road
USA	1101 CH Amsterdam	USA	#22-01 to #29-01
www.cisco.com	The Netherlands	www.cisco.com	Singapore 068912
Tel: 408 526-4000	www-europe.cisco.com	Tel: 408 526-7660	www.cisco.com
800 553-NETS (6387)	Tel: 31 0 20 357 1000	Fax: 408 527-0883	Tel: +65 6317 7777
Fax: 408 526-4100	Fax: 31 0 20 357 1100		Fax: +65 6317 7799

Cisco Systems has more than 200 offices in the following countries and regions. Addresses, phone numbers, and fax numbers are listed on the
Cisco.com Web site at www.cisco.com/go/offices.

Argentina • Australia • Austria • Belgium • Brazil • Bulgaria • Canada • Chile • China PRC • Colombia • Costa Rica • Croatia • Czech Republic
Denmark • Dubai, UAE • Finland • France • Germany • Greece • Hong Kong SAR • Hungary • India • Indonesia • Ireland • Israel • Italy
Japan • Korea • Luxembourg • Malaysia • Mexico • The Netherlands • New Zealand • Norway • Peru • Philippines • Poland • Portugal
Puerto Rico • Romania • Russia • Saudi Arabia • Scotland • Singapore • Slovakia • Slovenia • South Africa • Spain • Sweden
Switzerland • Taiwan • Thailand • Turkey • Ukraine • United Kingdom • United States • Venezuela • Vietnam • Zimbabwe

About the Author

Scott Bennett earned his CCNA, CCAI, and CompTia A+ while working and teaching in the technology industry. After graduating from Gonzaga University, Scott went on to work with Qwest eBits, providing network support and training to businesses throughout Idaho. His current position as a Cisco Networking Academy instructor for the Capital Center High School Technology Institute and Portland Community College provided the ideas and inspiration for this book.

About the Technical Reviewers

Mark R. Anderson, CCNA/CCNP, has been the lead Cisco Network Academy faculty at Mesa Community College in Mesa, Arizona since 1999. His 25+ years in the IT industry has given him invaluable experience in preparing and passing many technical certification exams, such as CCNA, CCNP, MCSE, and MCNE. As a teacher, his passion has been to help students develop and expand their professional growth in the IT industry. He earned a Bachelor of Education from Pacific Lutheran University and a Master of Liberal Studies in Information Networking and Telecommunication from Fort Hays State University. Mark lives in Gilbert, Arizona with Sandra, his wife of 35 years, and nearby adult children, Clint, Jennifer, and Trisha.

Glenn Wright, CCNA, CCAI, is the co-director of the Cisco Academy Training Center (CATC) in Ft. Worth, Texas. He has been involved in many aspects of the Cisco Networking Academy Program since 1999. He serves the Academy Program as an instructor and supports academies in Texas, Louisiana, Oklahoma, and Arkansas. Glenn has also worked with the Academy Quality Assurance Team, reviewing and editing Academy curriculum and assessment.

Dedication

To Grandpa Matt; my loving and supportive parents, Jim and Shari; my energetic and caring siblings, Jimmy, Johnny, Monnie, and Christi; and to Pam and George, for creating my beloved beautiful wife, Angie.

Acknowledgments

First, I want to thank Mary Beth Ray for her help in this process from start to finish. Her enthusiasm, professionalism, and ability to turn an idea into a proposal amaze me. Thank you for this remarkable experience and opportunity. Mark Anderson and Glenn Wright, thank you for your patience, wealth of knowledge, and attention to detail while editing the text. Chris Cleveland, thank you for pointing me in the right direction with the initial chapter and contributing the OSI model pneumonic device. Thank you to Dayna Isley for the innumerable improvements you contributed to the book and your positive encouragement. I greatly appreciate Allan Johnson's willingness to use a draft of the text in his CCNA review class and provide advice and assistance. Thank you to the entire Cisco Press team that worked behind the scenes to help create this book.

I also want to thank Matt Schoenfeldt for his continued and contagious eccentric passion about all things technical; Jeff Wirtzfeld for his support, supervision, and friendship at Qwest; Pete Craemer and David Gilde for their encouragement as fellow educators at the Capital Center High School; and Gary Schlienkofer for his aid with our Local Cisco Networking Academy. I would like to thank Trevor Hardcastle and Weiping He for keeping me on my toes as a teacher and in hopes that they might include my name in all of their future books. I also want to thank my friend Peter Buss for providing the perspective and empathy of a seasoned network administrator. Lastly, I want to thank Coach Dan Gehn, for teaching me the real meaning of the words *endurance* and *dedication,* and Professor Steven Gillick for his enthusiasm in the classroom and generous distribution of red ink on my papers.

Contents at a Glance

Contents

Day 2: Perform Simple WAN Troubleshooting   177

Day 1: Key Points from Each Day for Relaxed Skimming   181

Part V: Exam Day and Post-Exam Information   203

Exam Day: Becoming a CCNA   205

Post-Exam Information: After the CCNA   207

Index   211

Icons Used in This Book

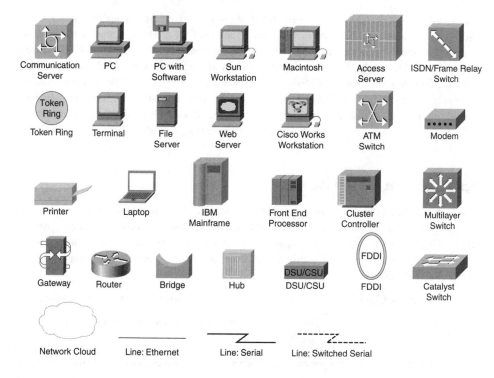

Command Syntax Conventions

The conventions used to present command syntax in this book are the same conventions used in the IOS Command Reference. The Command Reference describes these conventions as follows:

- **Boldface** indicates commands and keywords that are entered literally as shown. In actual configuration examples and output (not general command syntax), boldface indicates commands that are manually input by the user (such as a **show** command).

- *Italics* indicate arguments for which you supply actual values.

- Vertical bars (|) separate alternative, mutually exclusive elements.

- Square brackets [ ] indicate optional elements.

- Braces { } indicate a required choice.

- Braces within brackets [{ }] indicate a required choice within an optional element.

- A command that does not fit on one line due to the constraints of the book's width will continue on the next line with a two-space indent.

Introduction

31 Days Before Your CCNA Exam represents the end of your adventure through the Cisco
Networking Academy CCNA courses 1–4. Time to take the CCNA 640-801 exam and make your
knowledge official. You owe it to yourself to complete your academy studies with a CCNA certification. This book essentially offers a stepping-stone in what might otherwise feel like a big leap
between the Cisco Networking Academy curriculum and the CCNA exam. Each day breaks down
each exam topic into a manageable bite using short summaries from the online curriculum and a
conversational tone to make your study time more enjoyable. Use this book and its organized
course of study to take the guesswork out of your comprehensive academy review for the CCNA.

Goals and Methods

The main goal of this book is to provide you with a clear map from the Cisco Networking Academy
Program online curriculum to the CCNA exam. You will read short summaries of sections from the
Networking Academy online curriculum as they relate to each of the exam topics for the CCNA.
This book also outlines the format of the CCNA exam and the registration requirements you must
fulfill to take the CCNA exam.

Each day in the book uses the following formats to review the Networking Academy online curriculum:

- Short summaries of key concepts and definitions from the curriculum with a reference to the
  Networking Academy online module section number

- Tables and figures to help you recognize topics that you covered during your Networking
  Academy studies

- No-frills Cisco IOS software command-line examples to jog your memory about the configurations and lab exercises that relate to each CCNA objective

- References for further study and practice testing with the *CCNA Flash Cards and Exam
  Practice Pack* (CCNA Self-Study, exam #640-801), Second Edition (ISBN 1587200791) by
  Jim Doherty and Eric Rivard.

This book can also provide instructors and students with a concise way to review all four courses at
the end of a CCNA 4 class and add a little personality and a new angle to the Academy curriculum.
You can use this book to fit CCNA studies into an otherwise busy schedule with a daily timeline
and clear references to other CCNA study materials.

Who Should Read This Book?

The primary audience for this book is anyone teaching or enrolled in the Cisco Networking Academy
CCNA 4 WAN Technologies course or recent graduates of the Cisco Networking Academy CCNA
curriculum who have not yet passed the CCNA exam.

How This Book Is Organized

After you read through the instructions provided later in this introduction for registering for the CCNA exam, the books starts by breaking up the exam topics by day. The book counts down starting with Day 31 and continues through exam day to provide post-test information. The 31 days are broken into the four categories for the CCNA 640-801 exam: technology, planning and design, implementation and operation, and troubleshooting. Each day is titled with the CCNA exam objective, and each heading identifies the Networking Academy course (CCNA 1, CCNA 2, CCNA 3, or CCNA 4). Each subheading provides the module and section from the Networking Academy course and then provides a brief description of topics related to that day's exam objective.

At the end of the book, you will find a calendar and checklist that you can tear out and use during your exam preparation. Use the calendar to enter each actual date beside the countdown day and the exact day, time, and location of your CCNA exam. The calendar provides a visual for the time you can dedicate to each CCNA exam objective. You can also put a red X on each day you complete, like those movie montages where the lead character is preparing for something very important.

Use the checklist to map out your studies for the CCNA exam. The checklist highlights important tasks and deadlines leading up to your exam.

Look for daily reading quizzes and activities online. Visit the book's product page at www.ciscopress.com/title/1587131749 to access the content.

Study Tips

As you begin studying for the CCNA exam, you may find it helpful to buy a whiteboard. Get a dry erase marker and fill the room with that awful scent while you diagram and teach each of the concepts to yourself. Teach out loud. Teach whoever will listen. More important than anything, you need to inject yourself into this information. Your desire to get a CCNA and understand these concepts will shine through on test day. If you cannot explain and diagram an objective, then you do not know it. The real test happens when your boss asks you to explain a networking concept or to defend your suggestion in a meeting. The following activities could also help you to prepare:

- Podcast audio discussions about CCNA topics.

- Capture video lessons of yourself and watch them.

- Donate a set amount for every hour that you study to a children's hospital. Ask friends to sponsor you.

- Blog what you are learning.

- Get a copy of *CCNA Flash Cards and Exam Practice Pack* (CCNA Self-Study, exam #640-801), Second Edition (ISBN 1587200791), and tackle the suggested readings and practice exams for each day.

Getting to Know the CCNA Exam

The CCNA 640-801 tests your ability to describe, compare, connect, configure, and troubleshoot networks. Just knowing the information will help you on the exam, but also knowing the testing process, format, and environment will build your confidence and reduce the chance of any unpleasant surprises on exam day.

Exam Topics

The topics of the CCNA 640-801 exam focus around the following four key categories:

- **Technology**—The topics in this category relate to the theory and concepts behind networks, including layered models as well as network process descriptions.

- **Planning and design**—This category asks you to organize the concepts of networking into real-world examples.

- **Implementation and operation**—This category is where you prove that you can actually connect and configure a network.

- **Troubleshooting**—As a Cisco Networking Academy student, your networks are always perfect, but you need this category to fix networks affected by natural disasters, hardware issues, and the occasional malfunctioning keyboard during IP address configuration.

Each category includes general exam topics. In this book, each day represents a CCNA exam topic and each day maps the information you have learned in the Cisco Networking Academy Curriculum to a CCNA exam topic.

Although Cisco outlines general exam topics, it is possible that not all topics will appear on the CCNA exam and that topics that are not specifically listed may appear on the exam. The exam topics provided by Cisco and included in this book are a general framework for exam preparation. Be sure to check Cisco.com and look at the latest exam topics. You can navigate to CCNA information through the Learning and Events link.

Exam Format

For the CCNA exam, you are allowed 90 minutes to answer 55–65 questions. Table I-1 outlines each type of question that you might encounter on the exam.

Table I-1   CCNA Question Types

Question Type	Description
Multiple-choice single answer	You choose one and only one option for an answer.
Multiple-choice multiple answer	You choose more than one answer. The question itself will tell you how many answers you must select.
Drag-and-drop	You drag and release objects to visually arrange the answer on the page. These questions are similar to the drag-and-drop Interactive Media Activities in the Academy online curriculum.
Fill-in-the-blank	You click a text box and then type the answer. Sometimes there will be more than one text box.
Testlet	You see an upper pane and lower pane in the main window for this type of task. The upper pane contains a scenario, and the lower pane contains multiple-choice questions with single and multiple answers. On the right side, you can scroll through the scenario and select questions.
Simlet	A top window pane contains questions, and a bottom window pane contains a router simulation that you can use to answer the questions.
Simulations	This task is similar to the e-Labs that cover configurations. Remember that not all commands are supported in these simulations and that you can view the topology of the network in some simulations. You see the actual problem at the top and the directions on the left.

Cisco.com has an exam tutorial that simulates each of these types of questions. As you work through the exam tutorial, identify the question types that will take you longer to complete so that you can manage your time on exam day. The following steps allow you to access this tutorial:

Step 1.   Visit http://www.cisco.com.

Step 2.   Click the Learning and Events link.

Step 3.   Click the Career Certifications and Paths link.

Step 4.   Click the Certification Exam Information link.

Step 5.   Click the Certification Exam Tutorial link.

Your Path to the CCNA

As a Cisco Networking Academy student, you have a unique opportunity to integrate your final days of the study with preparation for the CCNA exam. Before you complete CCNA 4, you should plan to pass the CCNA voucher exam and take advantage of the practice and skills exams available through the Cisco Academy web site. It is important to schedule the following three exams with your Academy instructor in order to be best prepared for the CCNA:

- CCNA 640-801 Voucher Exam

- CCNA 640-801 Certification Practice Exam 1

- CCNA 640-801 Certification Practice Exam 2

After completing these exams, you can register to take the CCNA exam.

CCNA 640-801 Voucher Exam

Your instructor can activate and proctor this exam for you through the Cisco Academy web site during the CCNA 4 course. The default duration of the exam is 75 minutes, and the exam includes multiple-choice, single-answer and multiple-choice, multiple-answer questions. You have three attempts (each a different form of the exam) to complete with a score of "voucher eligible." The specific percentage that indicates "voucher eligible" is different for each form. Your voucher will be redeemable for a discount on the CCNA exam at a Prometric or Pearson VUE testing center. The discount percentage varies by region and testing center. If you pass the voucher exam and have successfully completed all final exams for The Cisco Networking Academy CCNA 1 through CCNA 4 with a 70 percent or better in the first attempt, you will be able to request a voucher from your Cisco Academy home page.

CCNA 640-801 Certification Practice Exams 1 and 2

The CCNA Certification Practice Exams 1 and 2 have between 55 and 60 questions, and you are allowed 120 minutes on each exam by default. You can take these exams up to ten times each. You must be enrolled in a CCNA 4 class and request that your instructor enable these practice exams in the Cisco Academy online assessment system.

Registering for the CCNA Exam

Once you have taken these exams and redeemed your voucher, you need to gather the information outlined in Table I-2 to register for the CCNA 640-801 exam.

Table I-2   Personal Information for CCNA 640-801 Exam Registration

Item	Notes
Legal name	
Social Security or passport number	
Cisco certification ID or test ID	
Cisco Academy username	Required for your voucher
Cisco Academy ID number	Required for your voucher
Company name	
Valid e-mail address	
Voucher number	Required for your voucher
Method of payment	Typically a credit card

You can register for an exam up to six weeks in advance or as late as the day before the exam. If you had an account with a testing partner before you began with the Academy, it is important to ensure that your profile is updated with your Academy information for the Academy voucher before you register. You can contact the testing partners in Table I-3 to register for an exam. The process and available test times will vary based on how and with whom you decide to register.

Table I-3   Test Delivery Partners

Testing Partner	Phone Number	Website
Pearson VUE	1-800-829-6387 option 1 then option 4	http://www.vue.com/cisco
Thomson Prometric	1-800-829-6387 option 1 then option 4	http://securereg3.prometric.com

There is no better motivation for study than an actual test date. *Sign up as soon as you have your voucher.*

Part I

31-24 Days Before the Exam—Technology

Day 31: Describe Network Communications Using Layered Models

Day 30: Describe the Spanning Tree Process

Day 29: Compare and Contrast Key Characteristics of LAN Environments

Day 28: Evaluate the Characteristics of Routing Protocols

Day 27: Evaluate the TCP/IP Communication Process and Its Associated Protocols

Day 26: Describe the Components of Network Devices

Day 25: Evaluate Rules for Packet Control

Day 24: Evaluate Key Characteristics of WANs

Describe Network Communications Using Layered Models

If the CCNA had a skeleton, networking models would be it. A solid understanding of these models prevents your network knowledge from resembling spineless, shapeless jelly. The networking models from CCNA 1 provide a framework for the concepts and configurations covered throughout the Cisco Networking Academy Program curriculum. Today you cover the Open System Interconnection (OSI) and TCP/IP layered models described in Modules 2, 6, 9, and 11 from CCNA 1 and the Cisco three-layer hierarchical model described in Module 5 from CCNA 3.

Do not stop with the quick summaries provided today. Look in the curriculum for related charts and graphics. Many other online resources, such as Wikipedia (www.wikipedia.com), also have excellent explanations. You might even have something to add to the Wikipedia explanations after your studies.

CCNA 1, Module 2

2.3.1—As you track the flow of information across a network, you will notice specific points where data changes on its route to a destination. The layers of the OSI and TCP/IP models help to explain why these changes occur and the process that helps the data find its way from one node to the next.

2.3.2—When two nodes communicate, they follow a protocol or an agreed upon set of rules to ensure the successful transmission of data. Keep in mind that peer layers communicate with each other.

2.3.3—Initially, companies developed proprietary network technologies that naturally caused compatibility issues, so the OSI model was released in 1984.

The benefits of using the OSI model to describe networks and networking devices are as follows:

- Reduces complexity
- Standardizes interfaces
- Facilitates modular engineering
- Ensures interpolable technology
- Accelerates evolution of networks
- Simplifies teaching and learning

2.3.4 and 2.3.5—Here is Yet Another OSI Model Chart (YAOMC). It wouldn't be a CCNA book without one. Table 31-1 describes each layer of the OSI model. Note that the protocol data unit (PDU) for each layer is in italics. A mnemonic such as Please Do Not Throw Sausage Pizzas Away might help you to remember each of the seven layers quickly for the exam.

Table 31-1   The Open System Interconnection Seven-Layer Model

Layer Number	Layer Name	Function	Devices
7	Application	E-mail, FTP, and other programs that allow the user to enter *data*.	N/A
6	Presentation	Encryption and compression can occur. *Data* is represented in a standard syntax and format such as ASCII.	N/A
5	Session	Set up, management, and tear down for sessions between programs exchanging *data*.	N/A
4	Transport	*Segments* are transported with reliability, error detection, and flow control.	N/A
3	Network	*Packets* are routed over the network and receive a path based on their IP address.	Router
2	Data link	*Frames* traverse the LAN with a MAC address as the identifier.	Bridge, switch
1	Physical	*Bits* physically pulse or wave their way over the network media representing 1s and 0s.	Hub, repeater, copper, optical, wireless

2.3.6—The TCP/IP model achieves the same main goals as the OSI model. The U.S. Department of Defense developed the model to define a network that could withstand nuclear war. Table 31-2 matches the layers of the TCP/IP model with the OSI model.

Table 31-2   The TCP/IP Model Versus the OSI Model

TCP/IP Model	OSI Model
4 Application	7 Application 6 Presentation 5 Session
3 Transport	4 Transport
2 Internet	3 Network
1 Network Access	2 Data link 1 Physical

2.3.7—The PDUs identified in the OSI model are encapsulated as they travel through the layers and from host to destination. In the top three layers, the data remains data. When data enters the transport layer, it is packaged into segments. The network layer then packages the segments into packets and adds a source and destination IP address. The data link layer packages the packet into a frame and adds a source and destination MAC address. Finally, the frame becomes a series of bits for transmission over the physical media.

CCNA 1, Module 6

6.1.3—The data link layer of the OSI reference model consists of two sublayers:

- The upper sublayer is the Logical Link Control (LLC) sublayer. The LLC sublayer communicates with the upper layers of the OSI model.

- The lower sublayer is the MAC sublayer. The MAC sublayer controls access to the physical media. 802.3 Ethernet operates in the physical layer of the OSI model and in the MAC sublayer of the data link layer.

6.1.5—Layer 2 frames are made up of fields. These fields allow the receiving host to identify the beginning, end, destination, and successful transfer of a frame. Without frames, the transmission would be just a big stream of ones and zeros. The fields in a generic frame are as follows:

- **Start of Frame**—This field identifies the beginning of a frame.

- **Address**—This field contains the source and destination MAC address.

- **Length/Type**—If this is a length field, it defines the length of the frame; if it is a type field, it identifies the Layer 3 protocol for the frame.

- **Data**—Where the data resides that is processed by the upper layers. (In this case, *upper layers* refers to Layers 3–7 in the OSI model and Layers 3 and 4 in the TCP/IP model.)

- **Frame Check Sequence**—This field provides a number that represents the data in the frame and a way to check the frame and get the same number. Cyclic redundancy check (CRC) is a common way to calculate the number and check for errors in the frame.

6.2.1—Three Layer 2 technologies that control how the physical media is accessed are Ethernet, Token Ring, and FDDI. As part of the MAC sublayer, these technologies can be divided into two groups: deterministic and nondeterministic. FDDI and Token Ring are deterministic in that they provide a way to take turns accessing the media. Ethernet is nondeterministic and uses carrier sense multiple access collision detect (CSMA/CD) as the protocol for accessing the media. This means that a node will first check to see if there is already a transmission and begin sending if the line is available. If two nodes transmit at the same time, a collision will occur and both nodes will wait a random amount of time before trying again.

CCNA 1, Module 9

9.1.1—Do not confuse the OSI and TCP/IP models despite the fact that some of the layers have the same name. The same layers in the different models have different functions. Unless otherwise noted, most CCNA questions will reference the OSI model. Pay close attention to the layer name and model name in any layered model question.

9.1.2—The application layer of the TCP/IP model includes programs and protocols that prepare the data to be encapsulated in the lower layers. Examples of these programs are as follows:

- FTP

- TFTP

- Simple Mail Transfer Protocol (SMTP)

- Simple Network Management Protocol (SNMP)

- Telnet

- Domain Name System (DNS)

9.1.3—TCP and UDP operate as protocols of the TCP/IP transport layer. Both TCP and UDP segment data from the TCP/IP application layer and send the segments to the destination host. UDP is a connectionless protocol that sends the data without verifying a successful transfer. TCP, however, ensures reliable transfer with acknowledgments and sequencing, provides flow control, and is classified as a connection-oriented protocol.

9.1.4—The TCP/IP Internet layer finds the path for packets over the network. This layer includes the connectionless protocol IP and Internet Control Message Protocol (ICMP). The TCP/IP internet layer also uses Address Resolution Protocol (ARP) to find a MAC address and Reverse Address Resolution Protocol (RARP) to find an IP address.

9.1.5—The TCP/IP network access layer, also called the host-to-network layer, provides the protocols to access the physical media and the standards for the media (wires, fiber, and radio frequency). Examples of these protocols are as follows:

- Ethernet

- Fast Ethernet

- Point-to-Point Protocol (PPP)

- FDDI

- ATM

- Frame Relay

9.1.6—Pay close attention to the fact that the application layer of the TCP/IP model includes the application, presentation, and session layers of the OSI model and that the TCP/IP network access layer includes the data link and physical layers of the OSI model. The OSI model appears more in academic and theoretical situations, whereas the TCP/IP model is the basis for development of the Internet. Know both models.

CCNA 1, Module 11

11.1.1—When you think about the transport layer, consider flow control and reliability. The transport layer achieves these goals through sliding windows, segment sequence numbers, and acknowledgments.

11.1.2—When two hosts establish a logical TCP connection at the transport layer, they agree on a reasonable flow of information. This flow control allows the receiving host to process the information in time to receive new segments from the sending host.

11.1.3—In order to start passing segments at the transport layer, two hosts must set up and maintain a session. The application initiating the connection and the operating system communicate with the receiving host's application and operating system to set up and synchronize a session. TCP avoids congestion at the transport layer by allowing the receiving host to send **ready** and **not ready** indicators to the sending host.

11.1.4—Applications that use the connection-oriented protocol TCP at the transport layer must first set up a session. Send a SYN, receive an ACK, send back an ACK +1, and you are connected using the TCP protocol. This three-way handshake defines the sequencing for TCP communication. Remember that both hosts must send an initial sequence number and receive an acknowledgment for communication to proceed.

11.1.5—TCP can play with these ACKs to define how much can be sent using sliding windows. A host initially sends a segment with a window size of 1. The receiving host could respond with an acknowledgment and identify that it would like a window size of 2. The sending host shoots back two segments and the receiving host acknowledges and asks for a window size of 3. If at some point during this transfer the receiving host does not acknowledge the transfer, the sending host tries again with a smaller window size. These sliding windows control flow between the two hosts.

11.1.6—How does the sending host know to retransmit a segment? As mentioned previously, retransmission occurs in the negotiation of a window size. To further explain the process, the sending host's need to retransmit relies on the numbers sent with acknowledgments. If a sending host fires segments 1, 2, and 3 over to the receiving host and receives an ACK 4, it knows to send segments 4, 5, and 6, as shown in Figure 31-1. If the receiving host were to return only an ACK 3, the sending host would have to retransmit segment 3. Try illustrating this process. (You can use the "Your Notes" section that appears after today's summary.) If you need help, visit module 11.1.6 in the CCNA 1 curriculum.

Figure 31-1   TCP Sliding Window

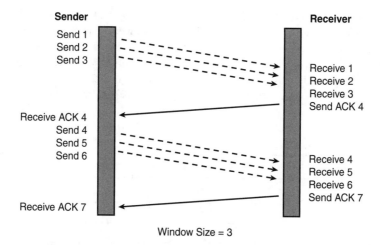

11.1.7—FTP, HTTP, SMTP, and Telnet use the transport layer TCP protocol. All of these protocols benefit from the connection-oriented, reliable transfer that TCP provides. The fields of a TCP segment are as follows:

- Source port

- Destination port

- Sequence number

- Acknowledgment number

- Header length (HLEN)

- Reserved

- Code bits

- Window

- Checksum

- Urgent pointer

- Option

- Data

11.1.8—TFTP, SNMP, DHCP, and DNS use the connectionless transport layer protocol UDP. UDP streams its segments at the receiving host and leaves the error checking to the upper-layer protocols. Notice in the following UDP fields that there are no acknowledgement, sequence, and window fields:

- Source port

- Destination port

- Length

- Checksum

- Data

11.1.9—If someone connects to your desktop on port 27015, you are likely hosting a video game. This port is not one of the well-known port numbers assigned by the Internet Assigned Numbers Authority (IANA) because it provides standard port numbers below 1024 for protocols such as FTP (port 21 TCP) and HTTP (port 80 TCP). The destination host must connect on a standard port number while the source host dynamically assigns a number above 1023 for the source port number. Memorize the common registered TCP and UDP port numbers for the protocols included in Table 31-3.

Table 31-3   Transport Layer Ports

Application Layer Protocol	Transport Layer Port/Protocol
http	Port 80 TCP
FTP	Port 21 TCP
Telnet	Port 23 TCP
SMTP	Port 25 TCP
DNS	Port 53 UDP and TCP
TFTP	Port 69 UDP
SNMP	Port 161 UDP
RIP	Port 520 UDP

11.2.1–11.2.7—Each of the application layer protocols in Table 31-4 provides a key function for Internet use.

Table 31-4   Application Layer Protocols

Protocol	Description
DNS	The DNS represents an IP address with a domain name. Each domain name has an extension such as .com that helps to identify the purpose of the site.
FTP and TFTP	FTP allows connection-oriented TCP-based file transfer between a client and a server. TFTP uses the connectionless UDP protocol to transfer files without the feature set of FTP. It is possible to transfer Cisco IOS images using TFTP.
HTTP	HTTP uses TCP and allows a user to navigate web sites on the Internet using a browser.
SMTP	SMTP uses TCP at OSI Layer 4 to send e-mail.
SNMP	SNMP allows an administrator to observe activity and troubleshoot problems on a network. A network management system can collect information provided by network devices.
Telnet	Telnet provides a command-line interface to a remote host.

CCNA 3, Module 5

5.2.1—Networking engineers use a three-layer hierarchical model to describe and design networks. This model consists of the core, distribution, and access layers, which provide an outline for the types of devices and connectivity necessary in a large network. The core layer serves as the backbone reserved for high-speed transmission. The distribution layer divides the core layer from the access layer and provides policy-based connectivity. The access layer connects users and remote sites to the network.

Summary

The OSI model and its seven layers cover each aspect of networking as data changes to segments, to packets, to frames, and then to bits. Only four layers comprise the TCP/IP model. The three-layer hierarchical model has three layers. In the "Your Notes" section that follows, it would be wise to diagram each of these layers and their characteristics from memory. If you have the *CCNA Flash Cards and Exam Practice Pack* (CCNA Self-Study, exam #640-801), Second Edition (ISBN: 1587200791), published by Cisco Press, now is a good time to review pages 13–34.

Your Notes

Describe the Spanning Tree Process

Switches can filter frames by MAC address and can speed up a network, but if you start to add backup connections to a switched network it is imperative to also run the Spanning Tree Protocol (STP). Module 8 from CCNA 1 and Module 7 from CCNA 3 describe STP and its operation.

CCNA 1, Module 8

8.1.6—Redundantly connected switches provide a valuable backup connection, but it is important that these backup connections do not cause loops. STP uses the spanning tree algorithm to turn off redundant connections until they are needed. Switches running STP send bridge protocol data units (BPDUs) out each port to identify and block redundant paths. All switch ports can transition from blocking to learning to listening and then to forwarding during this process.

CCNA 3, Module 7

7.2.1—Switches filter by MAC address, but if a switch does not know the destination MAC address of a frame, it broadcasts (floods) that frame out all ports except the receiving port. A switch can forward a frame forever. At Layer 2, a switch has no way of recognizing and discarding a frame that it has already received. To avoid loops, redundantly connected switches must create a logical tree over which to send frames using the spanning tree algorithm.

7.2.2—STP is defined by the IEEE 802.1d standard and identifies the shortest paths in a switched network to build a loop-free topology. The logical tree starts at the root bridge. As mentioned previously in the section "CCNA 1, Module 8" under 8.1.6, switches start out by sending BPDUs across the network that allow each switch to identify the root bridge and build a logical tree by turning off nondesignated ports and maintaining a single link with designated ports. If there are multiple LAN segments, switches that are closest to the LAN become designated switches to forward traffic from that LAN.

7.2.3—BPDUs spread across the network, switches block nondesignated ports, the logical tree is in place, and the network is converged. The network should now have only one root bridge per network and one designated port per segment. Each nonroot bridge will have one root port. Designated ports and root ports can forward data traffic. The designated port is the only port to forward STP traffic onto the segment under normal converged conditions.

7.2.4—To determine the root bridge, switches also send a bridge ID (BID) with BPDUs. A BID contains the bridge priority number (32768 by default) and the switch MAC address. The switch with the lowest BID becomes the root bridge. Each switch assumes that it is the root bridge and initially sends out its BID as the root ID. A switch that does not have the lowest BID will replace its ID as the root bridge with the lowest BID that it receives from other switches. To ensure that a certain switch becomes the root bridge, a network administrator needs to set the bridge priority number.

7.2.5—Table 30-1 defines the states that a switch port can cycle through when connected to a network. Remember that a switch port can also be administratively disabled.

Table 30-1   Spanning-Tree Port States

Port State	Description
Blocking	The port looks only at BPDUs.
Listening	The port checks for multiple paths to the root bridge and blocks all ports *except* the port with the lowest cost path to the root bridge.
Learning	The port learns MAC addresses but does not forward data.
Forwarding	The port learns MAC addresses, forwards data, and processes BPDUs.

7.2.6—If all switch ports on a network are only in blocking or forwarding mode, spanning tree has successfully set up a logical tree and the network has converged. A change in the physical topology of a network causes spanning tree recalculation to occur in order to once again achieve convergence.

7.2.7—IEEE 802.1d STP prevents switching loops, but IEEE 802.1w Rapid Spanning Tree Protocol (RSTP) does it faster. Point-to-point and edge-type links in RSTP can cycle directly from blocking (renamed discarding) to forwarding. RSTP can converge in 15 seconds, while STP takes up to 50 seconds.

Summary

To achieve convergence and a logical tree with no loops, switches use STP or RSTP. In your notes, try drawing three diagrams—one that explains how a switching loop could occur, one that explains identification of the root bridge (showing BIDs), and one that depicts a converged network with each port labeled. CCNA 3, Module 7, in the online curriculum has some great examples if you need help. If you have the *CCNA Flash Cards and Exam Practice Pack* (CCNA Self-Study, exam #640-801), Second Edition (ISBN: 1587200791), published by Cisco Press, you might thumb through pages 301–329. The small amount of material covered today also gives you an opportunity to take your first timed Networking Academy online CCNA practice exam. Dive in and make your best attempt with the understanding that it is your first attempt.

Your Notes

Compare and Contrast Key Characteristics of LAN Environments

From casinos in Las Vegas to basements filled with mouse-clicking gamers, you encounter LANs. How you characterize and define the physical and logical topologies of these LANs is the key to configuring and troubleshooting them. Modules 2 and 6 from CCNA 1, Module 1 from CCNA 2, and Modules 4 and 5 from CCNA 3 provide the information needed to properly characterize a LAN environment.

CCNA 1, Module 2

2.1.4—The terms to describe the physical topology of a network help you to explain how all the devices are connected. These terms include the following:

- **Bus**—All devices connected to one single arterial cable

- **Ring**—Each host connected to two other hosts forming a ring

- **Star**—All hosts connected to a hub or switch

- **Extended Star**—Hosts connected to a hub or switch that is in turn connected to a hub or switch

- **Hierarchical**—A pyramid of extended star networks all connecting to a main proxy that handles traffic at the top of the pyramid

- **Mesh**—All hosts directly connected to all other hosts

Logical topologies determine how the hosts communicate across the medium. The two most common logical topologies are token-passing or broadcast.

2.1.5—Networks need a set of rules to determine how they communicate. These rules are defined as protocols. Network protocols control the type of connection, how data is transferred, and how to handle errors.

2.1.6—Computers, network interface cards, peripheral devices, networking media, and network devices make up the main parts of a LAN. You most often use Ethernet, Token Ring, or FDDI in LAN technologies.

CCNA 1, Module 6

6.1.4—00-B0-D0-06-00-A3 is the 48-bit MAC address of the host that I am using to write this section. The IEEE assigned those first six hex numbers to Intel (the company that made the network card). Intel gets to assign the last six hex numbers, called the Organizational Unique Identifier (OUI). A MAC address can also be called a burned-in address (BIA). Each frame that a host sends over the LAN includes a destination MAC address. All hosts on that LAN drop the frame unless the destination MAC address in the frame matches the MAC address of the host.

6.1.6—Ethernet frames did not always have a length field. The original Digital Intel and Xerox (DIX) version of Ethernet (Ethernet II) not only combined the preamble and start of frame delimiter, but also listed the length/type field as just type. TCP/IP today uses a length/type field to identify upper-layer protocols in IEEE 802.3 Ethernet.

6.1.7—The fields of an Ethernet frame are as follows:

- An Ethernet frame begins with a preamble made up of alternating 1s and 0s.

- The Start of Frame delimiter identifies the end of the preamble with the byte 10101011.

- The Destination and Source Address fields are next.

- The Length/Type field follows. If the Length/Type field is less than 0x600 hex, it represents the length of the data in the next field. If the Length/Type field is greater than or equal to 0x600 hex, it represents the type of protocol; for example, 0x0800 hex is IP.

- The Data field contains information to be handled at the next layer.

- The Data field is followed by the Frame Check Sequence (FCS) field.

CCNA 2, Module 1

1.1.3—A LAN connects to other LANs and the Internet through a router. The router acts as the gateway for LAN devices and operates at Layer 3 of the OSI model. Routers communicate with each other to build routing tables allowing them to select the best path for a data packet between LANs. A router will only forward data outside of a LAN if it is destined for another network. This segments the LAN from other LANs and reduces overall traffic.

CCNA 3, Module 4

4.1.1—Ethernet 802.3 LANs started as simple networks connected with a hub or concentrator and evolved into sophisticated topologies operating on many layers of the OSI model. Initially, LANs connected using thick Ethernet and thin Ethernet using a bus topology. Hubs, or multiport repeaters, became common in networks as a way to retime and amplify signals to devices now connected in a star topology. All signals traveled over the hub network to all devices, so the potential for a collision existed on the entire network. Layer 2 bridges were introduced and did not just retime and regenerate the signals like a hub. Bridges were able to look at the MAC address and decide whether or not to forward a frame. Networks could now be divided into two separate collision domains. If you build a LAN today, you will likely connect devices with a switch. This switch, or multiport bridge, can filter each port based on the Layer 2 MAC address and provide a separate collision domain for each connected device. Switches and bridges do not filter broadcasts, so a Layer 3 router functions as the gateway that filters all LAN traffic and only forwards information destined for other connected LANs.

4.1.4—Shared Ethernet networks that operate in half-duplex can allow only one host to transmit or receive at a time. The collisions mentioned in this section under 4.1.1 occur when two devices attempt to transmit or receive at the same time. When this happens, the device that notices the collision sends a jam signal, and both devices wait a random amount of time (based on a backoff algorithm) before attempting to use the network again. On an Ethernet network, this is defined as carrier sense multiple access collision detect (CSMA/CD). The more devices you connect to a hub on a half-duplex network, the higher the potential for a collision. It would be difficult to sell IP phones to a school connected with all hubs, for example. Excessive collisions can congest a network.

4.1.6—Network latency slows connectivity and is an especially sour term for network gamers. The time it takes a network interface card (NIC) to receive or place a signal on a wire and the time it takes that signal to travel over the network contributes to latency. Layer 3 devices can increase latency because they take more time than a Layer 2 device to process network data.

4.1.9—As mentioned previously in this section under 4.1.1, switches can use MAC addresses to create direct virtual connections between two hosts on a network. This type of connection allows each of the two hosts to both transmit and receive at the same time. This full-duplex communication uses all the bandwidth in both directions, allowing for a 20 Mbps connection on a 10 Mbps network.

4.2.10—The latency caused by a switch relates directly to how it processes a frame. Switches can operate in cut-through or store-and-forward modes. Store-and-forward mode results in the switch receiving the *entire* frame before forwarding the information. In cut-through mode, a switch either sends the frame as soon as it knows the destination MAC address (fast-forward) or reads the first 64 bytes and then sends the frame (fragment-free).

4.3.2—In addition to cut-through or store-and-forward modes, switches can also operate in adaptive cut-through mode. This mode is a combination of cut-though and store-and-forward. Initially, the switch operates in cut-through until there are a certain number of errors that cause it to switch to store-and-forward.

4.3.5—Routers, bridges, and switches improve network functionality because they protect hosts from unnecessary traffic. Routers filter broadcasts and forward only packets that are destined for other networks to other ports. Switches divide collision domains and only pass frames over the wire to hosts with the proper destination MAC address.

4.3.7—The host-to-host virtual circuit that a switch creates can be referred to as microsegmentation. Because switches can microsegment networks into virtual circuits based on the MAC address filtering, each port on a switch is its own collision domain.

4.3.8—Remember that devices can send out Layer 2 broadcasts to contact all hosts with a destination MAC address of FF-FF-FF-FF-FF-FF. These frames are still broadcast to all hosts by switches. Switches do not divide broadcast domains. Without routers to filter these broadcasts, the Internet would be pretty darn slow.

CCNA 3, Module 5

5.1.2—When you design a LAN, consider how many hosts populate each collision and broadcast domain. Use switches to segment collision domains and routers to filter broadcasts. You will revisit all of Module 5 from CCNA 3 on Day 23, "Design a Simple LAN Using Cisco Technology."

Summary

LANs provide the local connectivity that supports business as well as important entertainment and therapeutic applications. How you use network devices and physical design to organize a LAN will decide the speed and efficiency of your network. In your notes you might sketch each of the physical and logical topologies that this chapter mentions. It would also help to quiz yourself on pages 36–60 of the *CCNA Flash Cards and Exam Practice Pack* (CCNA Self-Study, exam #640-801), Second Edition (ISBN: 1587200791), if you have one sitting near you.

Your Notes

Evaluate the Characteristics of Routing Protocols

Routing protocols are the legislators of the Internet. They constantly discuss and define the rules for what data goes where and what paths the data must take. Routing protocols can even have elections...kind of. Modules 6 and 7 from CCNA 2 and Modules 1, 2, and 3 from CCNA 3 shed light on the routing protocols that are important to passing the CCNA exam.

CCNA 2, Module 6

6.1.1—Routers choose a path over the network for a packet based on its destination IP address. How do routers know the best path for a packet? Either you tell them with a manually configured static route or the router uses a dynamic routing protocol to find out about the network topology and build its own routing table.

6.1.2—Once an administrator has configured a static route, the router adds that route to the routing table. The administrative distance for a static route is 1 by default. In the routing table, the route with the lowest administrative distance wins, so a 1 can only be bumped by a directly connected route with an administrative distance of 0. You can configure a static route as a backup route if you give it an administrative distance that is higher than a dynamic route in the routing table.

6.2.1—Routers use *routing protocols* to communicate with each other about networks and network locations. Examples of routing protocols include Routing Information Protocol (RIP), Interior Gateway Routing Protocol (IGRP), Enhanced Interior Gateway Routing Protocol (EIGRP), and Open Shortest Path First (OSPF). You must not confuse a routing protocol with a routed protocol. *Routed protocols* provide the information in a packet that allows the router to properly forward said packet. IP and Internetwork Packet Exchange (IPX) are examples of routed protocols.

6.2.2—Routing tables would be huge if there were no way to divide large networks into smaller groups of networks. Autonomous system (AS) numbers do just that with a 16-bit number assigned by the American Registry of Internet Numbers (ARIN). An AS number allows a network to represent itself as one unit.

6.2.3—Routers achieve convergence when all routers share a common view of the network via their routing table. If the network changes, routers must recalculate the routing tables using a dynamic routing protocol. AS numbers keep networks in manageable groups that allow routers to converge more quickly.

6.2.4–6.2.6—Routers can communicate about routes dynamically using one of the two classes of routing protocols in Table 28-1. Distance vector routing protocols look at how far away a route is and the direction (vector) to reach it. Link-state routing protocols build a topology of the entire network.

Table 28-1   Distance Vector and Link-State Protocols

Distance Vector	Link-State
Routers send periodic updates of the entire routing table to neighbors.	Routers send link-state advertisements (LSAs) to update other routers.
	Routers flood LSAs only when there is a topology change.
Routers see only neighboring routers.	Routers use the LSAs to build a full topology of the network.
Routers use a metric to determine the best path for a route and build a routing table.	Routers use the Shortest Path First (SPF) algorithm and LSAs to build a shortest path tree as well as a routing table.
	To develop a full loop-free topological database requires more memory than a distance vector protocol requires of a router.

6.3.1—When a router receives a packet on a port, it first looks at the destination address and compares it to its routing table. The router uses the routing table to determine the *best path* for the packet and forwards it out the appropriate port.

6.3.3—Each of the routing protocols described in Table 28-2 function at the Internet layer of the TCP/IP model. Border Gateway Protocol (BGP) is provided as an example of an exterior gateway protocol.

Table 28-2   Routing Protocols

Protocol Name	Type	Description
RIP	Distance vector	Broadcasts updates every 30 seconds and uses hop count as the metric with a maximum of 16
IGRP	Distance vector	Cisco proprietary protocol that broadcasts updates every 90 seconds and uses a composite metric of bandwidth, delay, load, and reliability
OSPF	Link-state	Nonproprietary protocol that updates only when there is a change in topology
EIGRP	Hybrid	Cisco proprietary protocol that uses both link-state and distance vector features and multicasts updates on 224.0.0.10
BGP	Exterior, distance vector	Used to route between autonomous systems

6.3.4—Table 28-2 shows how autonomous systems are able to communicate. If two networks, for example a company and an ISP, have different administrators and separate interior routing protocols, they can use BGP on their gateway routers to exchange information about directly reachable networks.

CCNA 2, Module 7

7.1.1–7.1.3—The key to finding the proper path, as mentioned previously, lies in the routing metric. Components of a routing metric could be any of the following:

- Internetwork delay
- Bandwidth
- Load
- Reliability
- Hop count

Routers using a distance vector routing protocol exchange routing tables with neighbors to learn the metric and best path. If these routers do not exchange routing tables quickly enough in a changing network, they can form a loop. A router on the network may not receive an update that a link is down and proceed to advertise that it can get to the network. If this router is able to update other routers with this information, the packets destined for the network could continue to pass around the network continuously. Distance vector routing protocols monitor the distance a packet travels as it passes over the network to avoid this type of loop. RIP tracks a packet with hop count and deems a network unreachable if it appears over 15 hops away. The maximum hop count of 16 ends the routing loop.

7.1.4–7.1.7—If routerA updates two connected routers that network1 is down but then accepts a later update from one of those same routers that network1 is reachable, you could have a loop. This scenario is possible because one of the connected routers may be getting old information from another part of the network originally sent out by routerA. Split horizon prevents this type of loop when it states that routerA cannot receive an update that concerns routes that routerA originally advertised. A router can also prevent loops by poisoning a route for a network that has gone down. A router can accomplish this by sending out the maximum hop count for a route as soon as it sees that the network is unreachable. This process is aptly named *route poisoning*. Typically, distance vector routing protocols update only on a set interval. This could cause routing issues if a network goes down and a router has to wait 30 seconds to send its next update. This problem is avoided with triggered updates. With route poisoning and triggered updates, a router ignores its regular schedule and shoots out the poisoned route information as soon as it notices that a network is down. This does not mean that routers immediately remove the route from the routing table; it just means that all routers know about the change. Routers implement a holddown timer that causes them to wait a set amount of time before actually removing a route from the routing table.

7.2.1—Linksys home router supports RIP, and for that matter many tombstones as well (bad joke). RIP is a distance vector routing protocol that implements split horizon and holddown timers. Each time a router running RIP receives an update, it adds a hop to the route to represent itself in the path to the destination. RIP will identify a network as unreachable if it has a hop count over 15. Routing updates occur every 30 seconds with RIP.

7.3.1 and 7.3.2—IGRP is also a distance vector routing protocol. Routing updates occur every 90 seconds with IGRP. IGRP focuses on speed as the main reason to use a particular route. The default metrics used by IGRP are bandwidth and delay, but IGRP can also be configured to use load and reliability. RIP uses only hop count as a metric to consider a path.

7.3.3 and 7.3.4—IGRP can advertise interior, system, and exterior routes. Interior routes are between networks that are connected to a router and have been divided into subnets. System routes are between networks inside of an autonomous system. Exterior routes define access to networks outside of an autonomous system. IGRP increases its stability as a routing protocol by using hold-down timers, split horizon, and poison reverse.

CCNA 3, Module 1

1.2.1–1.2.3—RIP, as mentioned previously in "CCNA 2, Module 7," is a distance vector routing protocol that uses hop count as a metric and implements both holddown timers and split horizon. RIP version 2 adds authentication and the ability to send a subnet mask with routing updates. This means that RIP version 2 supports variable-length subnet masks (VLSMs) and classless interdomain routing (CIDR). You will cover IP addressing and VLSM on Day 27, "Evaluate the TCP/IP Communication Process and Its Associated Protocols," and Day 22, "Design an IP Addressing Scheme to Meet Design Requirements." Another difference between RIP versions 1 and 2 is in how each protocol sends updates. RIP version 1 broadcasts updates on the address 255.255.255.255, whereas RIP version 2 more efficiently multicasts on the Class D address 204.0.0.9.

1.2.7—All routers on the Internet cannot contain a route for every network that exists. Routers can learn about other networks through static and dynamic routes, but for traffic destined outside of the immediate network an administrator can add a default route. A default route provides a destination for a router to forward all packets for which it does not have an entry in its routing table.

CCNA 3, Module 2

2.1.1–2.1.6—Table 28-1 implies that link-state routing protocols send updates only when the network changes. This is a partial truth. Sorry. Link-state protocols actually send little hellos periodically to obtain information about neighboring routers, but LSAs remain the key way that link-state protocols discover information across the entire network. When a network changes, a router will flood LSAs on a specific multicast address across the specified network area. These LSAs allow the router to create a topological database of the network, use the Dijkstra algorithm to determine the shortest path for each network, build the shortest path tree, and use the tree to build the routing table. Flooding LSAs across a network can affect overall bandwidth on a network and cause each router to recalculate a full topological database. For this reason, a network using a link-state protocol must be broken up into small enough areas to maintain network efficiency and use routers with sufficient memory and processing power.

2.2.1—OSPF is a nonproprietary link-state protocol that allows you to control the flow of updates with areas. OSPF proves itself a good choice for a large network because unlike RIP it allows more than 15 maximum hops and large networks can be divided into areas. These areas communicate with a backbone area to reduce routing protocol traffic and routing table size.

2.2.2–2.2.4—OSPF-enabled routers are true to their link-state definition in that they maintain a full loop-free topological database of the network. In addition to the topological database, each

OSPF-enabled router maintains a unique adjacency database that tracks only neighboring routers. OSPF-enabled routers also elect a designated router (DR) and backup designated router (BDR) as central points for routing updates. VLSM support, a bandwidth-based metric, a loop-free SPF tree, and rapid convergence through LSAs are key features of OSPF.

2.2.5—The OSPF adjacency databases are just great if you happen to be working with a Cisco Academy router pod with four routers each connected with point-to-point connections. Each router then will have two adjacencies: one for each directly connected neighbor. If you were to run OSPF on a fiber network, all routers would technically be connected on the fiber ring to each other. This means that each router would be a neighbor to every other router. OSPF avoids a network of never-ending neighbors with an election. Routers that are connected on broadcast multiaccess networks like fiber, Ethernet, or nonbroadcast multiaccess networks such as Frame Relay elect a single router called the DR to handle updates. To avoid a single point of failure, they also elect a BDR.

2.2.6—Those little OSPF hello packets typical to link-state protocols go out over the multicast address 224.0.0.5. If the connection is broadcast or point-to-point, the hellos default to 10 seconds, and if the connection is nonbroadcast multiaccess (NBMA), the packets default to 30 seconds. The contents of the hello packet include the following:

- Version

- Type

- Packet length

- Router ID

- Area ID

- Checksum

- Authentication type

- Authentication data

2.2.7—The OSPF process starts with hello packets to find neighboring routers and develop adjacencies. Routers first determine if they are on a point-to-point link or multiaccess link. If they are on a multiaccess link, a DR and BDR election occurs. Once adjacencies exist between neighbors, the routers forward LSAs and add information to their topological databases. Once the topological databases are complete, the routers use the SPF algorithm to create the SPF tree and then a routing table. Periodic hello packets can alert routers to a change in the topology that would restart the process.

CCNA 3, Module 3

3.1.1—EIGRP and IGRP routing protocols function seamlessly together despite the fact that EIGRP offers multiprotocol support and functions as a hybrid routing protocol. EIGRP also supports VLSM, whereas IGRP does not. A router running only IGRP will see EIGRP routes as IGRP routes.

3.1.2—As a hybrid multiprotocol routing protocol, EIGRP uses functions from both link-state and distance vector protocols. Like OSPF, EIGRP collects multiple databases of network information to build a routing table. EIGRP uses a neighboring table in the same way that OSPF uses an adjacency database to maintain information on adjacent routers. EIGRP, however, uses a distance vector diffusing update algorithm (DUAL) to recalculate a topology. EIGRP also maintains a topology table that contains routes learned from all configured network protocols. In the topology table, EIGRP defines the following fields:

- **Feasible Distance (FD)**—The lowest cost to each destination

- **Route Source**—The router identification number for externally learned routes

- **Reported Distance (RD)**—A neighboring router's reported distance to a destination

- **Interface Information**—Which interface to use to reach a destination

- **Route Status**—The status of a route, where ready-to-use routes are identified as passive and routes that are being recalculated are identified as active

The neighbor and topology table allows EIGRP to use DUAL to identify the best route, or the *successor route*, and enter it into the routing table. Backup routes, or *feasible successor routes*, are kept only in the topology table. If a network goes down and there is no feasible successor, the router sets the route to active, sends query packets out to neighbors, and begins to rebuild the topology. In the topology table, EIGRP can also tag routes as internal or external. Internal routes come from inside the EIGRP AS, and external routes come from other routing protocols and outside the EIGRP AS.

3.1.3 and 3.1.4—Advanced features of EIGRP that set it apart from other distance vector routing protocols include:

- **Rapid convergence**—EIGRP uses the DUAL finite-state machine (FSM) to develop a full loop-free topology of the network allowing all routers to converge at the same time.

- **Efficient use of bandwidth**—EIGRP, like OSPF, sends out partial updates and hello packets, but these packets go only to routers that need the information. EIGRP also develops neighboring relationships with other routers.

- **Support for VLSM and CIDR**—EIGRP sends the subnet mask information allowing the network to be divided beyond default subnet masks.

- **Multiple network layer support**—Rather than rely on TCP/IP to send and receive updates, EIGRP uses the reliable transport protocol as its own proprietary means of sending updates.

- **Independence from routed protocols**—EIGRP supports IP, IPX, and AppleTalk. EIGRP has a modular design that uses protocol-dependant modules (PDMs) to support other routing protocols, so changes to reflect revisions in the other protocols have to be made only to the PDM and not EIGRP.

3.1.5—EIGRP uses five different types of packets to communicate with other routers:

- **Hello**—Sent on 224.0.0.10 to communicate with neighbors

- **Acknowledgment**—Hello packets without data sent to acknowledge receipt of a message

- **Update**—Used to update new neighbors so that they can in turn update their topology

- **Query**—Used to gather information from one or many neighbors

- **Reply**—Sent as response to a query packet

3.1.6—As described in CCNA 3 Module 3.1.2, EIGRP-enabled routers build a topology table that contains and uses the DUAL algorithm to select the successor routes that will populate the routing table. If a link goes down, the DUAL algorithm selects a feasible successor from the topology table and promotes it to the successor route. If there is no feasible successor, EIGRP recalculates the topology table. This process and the DUAL algorithm enable EIGRP to achieve rapid convergence.

Summary

Make sure you know the difference between a distance vector routing protocol and a link-state protocol. It is not uncommon for the CCNA exam to test your understanding of routed vs. routing protocols as well. If you understand routing protocols, you know how it is possible for the Internet to function and send so much data to so many hosts. If you happen to see a copy of *CCNA Flash Cards and Exam Practice Pack* (CCNA Self-Study, exam #640-801), Second Edition nearby, you might flip through pages 388–450 and focus on the details of routing protocols. You can focus on the commands on a later day.

Your Notes

Evaluate the TCP/IP Communication Process and Its Associated Protocols

Network administrators, video game developers, and even the recording industry have taken great interest in the TCP/IP communication process. TCP/IP is the postal system that allows devices on the Internet to differentiate between one host and the next. Modules 1, 2, 9, 10, and 11 from CCNA 1 and Modules 8 and 10 from CCNA 2 outline the TCP/IP process and the associated protocols. You will quickly review some concepts from Day 31, "Describe Network Communications Using Layered Models," as well as learn new information. Expect more on IP addressing on Day 22, "Design an IP Addressing Scheme to Meet Design Requirements."

CCNA 1, Module 1

1.2.5 and 1.2.6—Understanding binary is important in order to understand IP addressing. Sometimes you will need to convert an IP address to its binary format when developing an IP addressing scheme for a network. Decimal to binary conversion requires that you determine what bits contain a 1 and what bits contain a 0. Table 27-1 shows the powers of 2 for each bit from left to right and the decimal equivalent in the other section. Look at how the two columns relate and see if you can complete the last two rows.

Table 27-1   Binary to Decimal Conversion

Bits and Powers of 2								Decimal Equivalent
1	1	1	1	1	1	1	1	128+64+32+16+8+4+2+1 = 255
128	64	32	16	8	4	2	1	
1	0	0	1	0	0	1	1	128+16+2+1 = 147
128	64	32	16	8	4	2	1	
0	1	1	0	0	0	1	0	
128	64	32	16	8	4	2	1	
-	-	-	-	-	-	-	1	
128	64	32	16	8	4	2	1	128+2+1 = 131

1.2.7, 1.2.9, and 1.2.10—A 32-bit IP address is made up of four sets of numbers, or octets. Each octet contains an 8-bit binary number like those shown in Table 27-1. When a router receives an IP address in a packet, the router uses Boolean logic to compare the IP address to the subnet mask and determine the network address. Boolean logic compares two numbers and provides a result based on the AND operator. Table 27-2 shows the rules for the AND operator and gives an example of applying an AND operation to an IP address and subnet mask to determine the network address.

Table 27-2   Using the AND Operator to Determine a Network Address

AND operator	IP Address and Subnet Mask to Network Address
0 AND 0 = 0	IP address 192.168.1.7 Mask 255.255.255.0
0 AND 1 = 0	IP address 11000000.10101000.00000001.00000111
1 AND 0 = 0	Subnet mask 11111111.11111111.11111111.00000000
1 AND 1 = 1	Result 11000000.10101000.00000001.00000000
	Network address 192.168.1.0

CCNA 1, Module 2

2.3.6 and 2.3.7—Table 27-3 summarizes the information presented from Day 31 about the layers of the TCP/IP model as compared to the OSI model, as well as the protocol data units (PDUs) used in each layer.

Table 27-3   The TCP/IP Model Versus the OSI Model, and the Corresponding PDU

TCP/IP Model	OSI Model	PDU
4 (application)	Application (Layer 7)	Data
	Presentation (Layer 6)	
	Session (Layer 5)	
3 (transport)	Transport (Layer 4)	Segments
2 (internet)	Network (Layer 3)	Packets
1 (network access)	Data Link (Layer 2)	Frames
	Physical (Layer 1)	Bits

CCNA 1, Module 9

9.1.1–9.1.6—As covered on Day 31, the TCP/IP model is made up of four layers. The application layer includes protocols such as FTP, TFTP, SMTP, and DNS. TCP and UDP operate at the transport layer. IP operates at the Internet layer and includes Ethernet, Frame Relay, PPP, ATM, and FDDI, as well as IEEE specifications for physical media. The TCP/IP model is the basis of the Internet, but the OSI model is often used in academic and theoretical situations because it further divides the networking process.

9.1.7–9.2.3— The Internet is made up of thousands of internetworks connected by routers through various types of physical media. To identify networks and get information to hosts, routers use the Internet Protocol (IP). MAC addresses work wonders on a LAN at Layer 2 to identify computers for switching. On multiple LANs divided by Layer 3 routers, however, IP addressing goes beyond unique identification to provide grouping by networks. This allows a router to keep a shorter table of network locations and not individual IP addresses. Each host on a network has a 32-bit address that is represented in dotted decimal format. Table 27-2 provides you with an example of an IP address represented in both dotted decimal and binary formats. Despite the fact that binary looks cooler, dotted decimal is easier to read. As shown in Table 27-4, converting binary IP addresses to decimal and back is all about the powers of two. Know those first 8 powers of 2 and you will be able to diagram an IP address as binary or decimal. It might also be good to practice adding those numbers in various combinations.

Table 27-4   One Octet of an IP Address

Bits and Powers of 2								Decimal Equivalent
1	1	1	1	1	1	1	1	128+64+32+16+8+4+2+1 = 255
128	64	32	16	8	4	2	1	

So how does an IP address display information about the specific host and the network? Part of an IP address represents the host, and part represents the network.

9.2.4—IP addressing is by default broken up into a set of classes that define the network and host portions. The first few binary digits in an IP address define the default address class. Table 27-5 provides as much information as will fit about address classes.

Table 27-5   Class A, B, C, D, and E IP Addresses

Class	Binary Start	1st Octet Range	Network (N) and host (H) Octets	Number of Hosts	Bits in Network Address
Class A	0	1–126	N.H.H.H	About 16 million	8
Class B	10	128–191	N.N.H.H	65,535	16
Class C	110	192–223	N.N.N.H	254	24
Class D	1110	224–239	H.H.H.H	Multicast	28
Class E	1111	240–255	RESEARCH	RESEARCH	RESEARCH

The Class A address 127.0.0.0 is reserved for the loopback.

9.2.5—The address for a network cannot be assigned to a host. This is like putting the name of your city on an envelope to represent where your house is located. The network address for a specific network is where the host portion is made up entirely of binary 0s. The broadcast address, or the address on a network used to reach all hosts on that network, cannot be assigned to a specific host. The broadcast address for a network is where the host portion is made up entirely of binary 1s. Table 27-6 shows a network and broadcast address example.

Table 27-6   Network and Broadcast Address Example

Network Default Class C	Binary Host All 0s Network Address	Binary Host All 1s Broadcast Address	Useable Hosts
192.168.1.0	192.168.1.0	192.168.1.255	192.168.1.1 to 192.168.1.254

9.2.6—Hosts that are directly connected to the Internet require a unique public IP address. Two hosts cannot have the same IP address on the Internet and expect traffic to route. For networks that are not connected to the Internet or that are using a proxy (covered on Day 20, "Design a Simple Internetwork Using Cisco Technology"), private or internal addresses are available as outlined in RFC 1918 and Table 27-7.

Table 27-7   Private Network Addresses

Class	Address Range
Class A	10.0.0.0 to 10.255.255.255
Class B	172.16.0.0 to 172.31.255.255
Class C	192.168.0.0 to 192.168.255.255

9.2.7—There are no networks in the world with 1 router and 16 million hosts. Class A networks are always divided, or subnetted in smaller subnetworks. The same is true of a network of any size that does not need to use the address space it reserves. If you have an entire class B network, you can increase the subnet mask by borrowing bits from the host portion and create multiple smaller networks. This is also possible with a class C network, and we will cover subnetting in depth on Day 22.

9.2.8—The IP address discussion to this point has been about 32-bit IP version 4 (IPv4) addressing. As IP addresses become scarce, it is possible that 128-bit IP version 6 (IPv6) addressing will become the leading protocol on the Internet. 128-bit IPv6 addresses consist of eight 16-bit sections separated by a colon and represented in hexadecimal format. With IPv6, the Internet has a potential 640 sextillion unique addresses.

9.3.1–9.3.5—You can assign a static IP address to a host, or the host can dynamically acquire an address. Servers and network devices that provide services to hosts should have a static IP so that the hosts can find them. Three common methods that hosts use to obtain an IP address automatically are as follows:

- **Reverse Address Resolution Protocol (RARP)**—Hosts can use RARP to associate a MAC address to an IP address. A RARP server, usually the router, must be present for RARP to function.

- **Bootstrap Protocol (BOOTP)**—BOOTP is a way for a host to use UDP to obtain an IP address as well as router and server information. You have to add an entry to the database on the BOOTP server for each host on the network.

- **DHCP**—DHCP does not require you to enter information for each host that you add to the network. As the replacement for BOOTP, DHCP requires only that you to enter a range (or pool) of IP addresses for the DHCP server to lease to a host. When the lease expires, the DHCP server can reclaim the address for other hosts.

9.3.6 and 9.3.7—RARP finds an IP using the MAC address, so Address Resolution Protocol (ARP) finds a MAC address using the IP address. ARP occurs when a host has a destination IP address for a packet but needs to determine the MAC address to send the packet over the LAN. Let's say hostA broadcasts an ARP request and hostD has the matching IP address. HostD will respond with its MAC address. HostA can then add this information to its ARP table and send the packet with the MAC-IP pair. If hostD is not on the local LAN, the router will recognize this and respond with its MAC address with the intent of forwarding the packet.

CCNA 1, Module 10

10.1.1–10.1.4—IP is a Layer 3 routed connectionless protocol. IP is considered a best-effort delivery system because it does not verify that a packet has reached its destination. If a packet does not reach its destination, an upper-layer protocol will request retransmission. A packet will maintain the same destination IP address as it travels across LANs, but each router that views and forwards the packet will strip and replace the Layer 2 destination MAC address to get the frame across the LAN. Remember that a Layer 3 packet is encapsulated in a frame for Layer 2 transport across a LAN. As a connectionless protocol, IP is a packet-switched process. Packet-switched communication can send packets along different network paths to be sorted and sequenced upon arrival at the destination. A circuit-switched connection sends packets in order across a physical or virtual circuit.

10.1.5—The following fields make up an IP packet:

- **Version**—Defines the format of the packet

- **IP Header Length (HLEN)**—Length of all header information

- **Type of Service**—Importance level as assigned by an upper-layer protocol

- **Total Length**—Length of the entire packet

- **Identification**—The sequence number

- **Flags**—Identifies if the packet can be fragmented and if it is the last piece of a fragmented packet set

- **Fragment Offset**—Used to assemble packet fragments

- **Time to Live (TTL)**—The number of hops a packet can travel before being discarded

- **Protocol**—Upper-layer protocol such as TCP or UDP

- **Header Checksum**—Used to check the header

- **Source Address**—IP address of sender

- **Destination Address**—IP address of intended recipient

- **Options**—Support for options like security

- **Padding**—Used to keep the IP header a multiple of 32 bits

- **Data**—Encapsulated information from upper layers, which can be up to 64 bits

CCNA 1, Module 11

11.1.1–11.2.7—Didn't we already cover Module 11 on day 31? Yep. Here are two quick paragraphs to summarize what Day 31 covered.

The TCP/IP transport layer creates a session between hosts using segments as the PDU and either standard ports (1023 and below) or nonstandard ports (above 1023). The TCP/IP transport layer can use TCP as a connection-oriented protocol, which features a three-way handshake, sliding windows, positive acknowledgement, and segment sequencing. Examples of protocols that use TCP are HTTP on port 80, FTP on port 21, and Telnet on port 23.

The TCP/IP transport layer can also use the connectionless UDP protocol, which does not feature acknowledgments or sequencing and broadcasts segments. Examples of protocols that use TCP are TFTP on port 69, SNMP on port 161, and RIP on port 520.

CCNA 2, Module 8

8.1.1–8.1.9—As mentioned previously, IP does not report errors in transmission. This is the job of the Layer 3 protocol Internet Control Message Protocol (ICMP). ICMP allows a router to send an error notification to the device that originally sent the packet. ICMP packets that cannot be delivered do not generate their own error messages to avoid congestion. The **ping** command uses an ICMP echo request to verify connections and waits to receive an ICMP echo reply. ICMP messages start with Type, Code, and Checksum fields. If a router cannot deliver a packet, it will provide an ICMP destination unreachable message with a specific code to identify why the destination is unreachable.

8.2.1–8.2.9—ICMP also sends control messages to tell hosts about network conditions. Different types of control messages are as follows:

- **ICMP redirect/change requests**—Allow a gateway to inform a host about a better route

- **ICMP timestamp messages**—Allow a host to exchange time information with a remote host and identify the delay across the network for time synchronization

- **ICMP source quench messages**—Allow a gateway to notify a host if the network is congested and to temporarily slow transmission

Hosts can also use ICMP to obtain an IP address to discover the subnet mask and to discover a router. In today's networks, hosts use DHCP to obtain IP addresses.

CCNA 2, Module 10

10.1.1–10.2.6—Although ICMP can send source quench messages, the real flow control happens at the transport layer with TCP. Module 10 in CCNA 2 repeats information from Module 11 in CCNA 1 and adds the following information:

- While a TCP connection is established using the three-way handshake, it is possible that a 1337hax0r (elite hacker) could send a number of SYN requests from a nonexistent IP address to this host. These repeated requests could cause a device to wait for an acknowledgement and use all of its resources. This type of denial-of-service (DoS) attack could prevent a device from responding to legitimate requests. Software exists that can recognize and repel such an attack.

- The process in sliding windows where TCP requests that a host resend information is called positive acknowledgement and retransmission (PAR).

- A more concise definition of port number ranges includes well-known ports (0 to 1023), registered ports (1024 to 49151), and dynamic ports (49152 to 65535).

- A host can provide services simultaneously on two different ports. An example might be a web server that provides HTTP access on port 80 at the same time as Telnet access on port 23.

- Port number assignment occurs at Layer 4 of the OSI model, IP address assignment occurs at Layer 3, and MAC address assignment occurs at Layer 2.

Summary

From the initial ARP request to find a destination IP address to the last acknowledgement of a TCP segment, the TCP/IP process assists Internet communication worldwide. It is important to understand the hierarchy and grouping of Layer 3 IP addresses and networks as well as the Layer 4 flow control and reliability of TCP. Pages 123–145 in the *CCNA Flash Cards and Exam Practice Pack* (CCNA Self-Study, exam #640-801), Second Edition (ISBN: 1587200791) might help you to refine this knowledge. Ignore the subnetting questions until after Day 22.

Your Notes

Describe the Components of Network Devices

Although protocols and software determine the logical layout and provide instructions for network processes, the engine of any network is its hardware. Modules 1 and 2 from CCNA 2 describe the various bits and pieces that make up network devices and how Cisco IOS software works with the hardware. On this short day you could definitely knock out another practice CCNA test when you have finished reading.

CCNA 2, Module 1

1.1.2 and 1.2.1—The internal components of a router are as follows:

- **Central processing unit (CPU)**—Runs instructions from the operating system, including initialization, routing, and interface control.

- **Random-access memory (RAM)**—Where the router stores routing table information and the running configuration, and where interfaces temporarily store packets that the router is forwarding. RAM loses all data when the router is powered off. The RAM can be upgraded with dual inline memory modules (DIMMs).

- **Flash**—Stores the full Cisco IOS software and can be upgraded with single inline memory modules (SIMMs) or a Personal Computer Memory Card International Association (PCMCIA) card.

- **Nonvolatile random-access memory (NVRAM)**—Stores the startup configuration and does not lose data when the router is powered down.

- **Buses**—The system bus is the internal means of communication between the CPU and other internal components. The CPU bus is used specifically for the CPU to transfer data to memory and back.

- **Read-only memory (ROM)**—Holds the ROM monitor, which runs hardware diagnostics, loads the IOS, and can contain a reduced version of the IOS for troubleshooting. The ROM can only be upgraded by replacing the actual chip.

- **Interfaces**—Connections from routers to other devices for networking and management.

- **Power supply**—Can be modular and supplies power to the router.

1.2.3–1.2.7—The following list describes the three ways (aside from power) that you can physically connect to a router:

- **LAN connections**—Ethernet, FDDI, and Token Ring technologies connect to a LAN interface. You need a straight-through cable to connect a router to a switch and a crossover cable to connect a router directly to a computer or another router.

- **WAN connections**—If you choose to connect to a WAN, the service provider will use a data circuit-terminating equipment or data communications equipment (DCE) device, which can be a channel service unit/data service unit (CSU/DSU) or a modem, to connect to your router as the data terminal equipment (DTE) device. The service provider uses the DCE device to set clocking on the connection.

- **Management ports**—Serial EIA-232 interfaces provide an out-of-band way to connect a terminal to the router and troubleshoot in a text-based session. Typically, you can use a rollover cable and a terminal emulation program (such as HyperTerminal) on a desktop computer to connect to the console port and manage a router. A quick and almost poetic way to remember the standard terminal configuration is to recall *9600-8-none-1-none*. You can also configure a router by dialing to a modem connected to the AUX port.

CCNA 2, Module 2

2.1.1–2.1.3—You can manage a router in a text-based terminal using a command-line interface (CLI). Initially, you connect physically to gain access, but once networking and virtual terminal access is configured you can also telnet to a router. Once you are logged in, the CLI has two key modes:

- User EXEC mode does not allow configuration changes and is represented by the hostname> prompt.

- Privileged EXEC mode gives you administrative access to all the configuration modes and is represented by the hostname# prompt.

2.1.4—Software compatibility with hardware comes into play when deciding to upgrade the Cisco IOS image on a router. An IOS image is named using a format that identifies first the platform, then the feature set, and lastly where the image will run and if it uses compression. The following list explains the components of the Cisco IOS image name *C2600-is-mz*:

- *C2600* refers to the platform, which is Cisco 2600 series.

- *is* refers to the feature set, which is IP Plus.

- *mz* refers to the image location/compression, which is RAM/zipped.

It is important to check your router to make sure that it has enough RAM and flash memory to support a new IOS image. You can look at this information in the CLI under user EXEC mode by typing **show version** to see the existing image name, amount of RAM, and amount of flash memory.

2.1.5—When you start a router, it can enter three different operating environments, as follows:

- **ROM Monitor (ROMMON)**—Used for password recovery and diagnostics. The prompt is a > or ROMMON>

- **Boot ROM**—A paired-down version of the IOS used to copy a new image to flash memory

- **Cisco IOS**—The full Cisco IOS image stored in flash

2.2.1—When a Cisco router powers up, it first performs a power-on self test (POST) and then it loads a bootstrap and initializes the Cisco IOS image from flash, a TFTP server, or ROM. The location of the IOS image can be specified in the configuration register. Once the IOS image is loaded, it loads the configuration file from NVRAM. If there is no configuration file in NVRAM, the IOS software searches for a TFTP server to load the configuration file. If there is no TFTP server, the IOS software starts the setup dialog.

2.2.2—A router has an LED light next to each interface that should blink to show activity if the interface is working properly. Next to the AUX port is an OK LED that illuminates when the system has initialized.

2.2.4—For a console TIA/EIA-232 port connection on a router, you use the RJ45 connector on one end of your console cable and the RJ45 to DB-9 adapter and serial COM port on your desktop. Once you have everything connected, open HyperTerminal and make sure that the settings are 9600-8-none-1-none.

Summary

Your experience with actual routing hardware from the Academy and knowledge of how the software and hardware in a router relate will help with any CCNA questions covering this objective. It might also help to look at many of the questions in pages 199–205 and 259–274 in the *CCNA Flash Cards and Exam Practice Pack* (CCNA Self-Study, exam #640-801), Second Edition (ISBN: 1587200791) and, of course, to take a quick practice CCNA exam today if you have time.

Your Notes

Evaluate Rules for Packet Control

The rules of Carrier Sense Multiple Access/Collision Detection (CSMA/CD) at Layer 2 and access control lists (ACLs) at Layer 3 help control how data can be sent across a network. Module 6 from CCNA 1 and Module 11 from CCNA 2 describe collision detection and Layer 3 ACLs. You will cover ACLs again on Day 19, "Develop an Access List to Meet User Specifications," Day 10, "Implement an Access List," and Day 3, "Troubleshoot an Access List."

CCNA 1, Module 6

6.2.2—CSMA/CD provides the rules for how a device can communicate on an Ethernet network. As discussed on Day 31, "Describe Network Communications Using Layered Models," a host listens to find out whether the network is available and then transmits data. If two hosts attempt to transmit at the same time, a collision occurs and both hosts transmit until all devices have detected the collision. All hosts then use the backoff algorithm to wait a random amount of time before attempting to retransmit.

6.2.6–6.2.8—The following are three main types of collisions that can occur on a network:

- **Local collision**—Occurs when a network card notices that the receive (Rx) wires detect a signal at the same time the transmit (Tx) wires attempt to send data.

- **Remote collision**—Occurs when a frame is too small. A remote collision is likely the result of a local collision on the other side of a hub or repeater. The repeater would only regenerate a fragment of the collision and not the simultaneous Tx and Rx.

- **Late collision**—Occurs after the first 64 bits of data have been transmitted for a frame. The Layer 2 network card cannot recognize this type of collision and must rely on the upper layers to request retransmission.

A *runt* is a frame that is less than the minimum size of 64 octets. These frames are usually collision fragments. A frame that exceeds the maximum legal frame size causes a network diagnostic tool to report jabber on the connection. If a frame does not match its own frame check sequence (FCS), this is considered a cyclic redundancy check (CRC) error.

CCNA 2, Module 11

11.1.1 and 11.1.2—If you configure an ACL on a router, the router checks each packet that it processes against the ACL. ACLs can provide instructions for a router to accept or deny a packet. An ACL can match a packet by source, destination, upper layer protocols, and port number. As an administrator, you can assign one outbound and one inbound ACL per port for each protocol. Key points to remember about an ACL include the following:

- To revise an ACL, you must delete and recreate the entire ACL.

- A router checks ACL statements in the order in which the ACL rules have been entered in the configuration. The router stops at the first match and does not check any other statements.

- At the end of every ACL there is an implicit deny that drops any packets that did not match an entry. We will cover configuration on Day 10, but remember that you need to add a permit statement at the end if you want a packet that matches no specific statements to be forwarded.

11.1.4—With a wildcard mask you can tell the router exactly what IP address or IP address grouping you want to filter. You pair a wildcard mask with an IP address and use binary to identify what part of the address should be matched. A binary 0 in a wildcard mask says that the bit should be matched. A binary 1 says that the bit can be ignored. Table 25-1 provides an example.

Table 25-1   A Wildcard Mask to Identify What an ACL Should Match

	Decimal	Binary[*]
IP Address	192.168.1.7	11000000.10101000.00000001.00000111
Wildcard Mask	0.0.0.255	00000000.00000000.00000000.11111111
Result	192.168.1.0	11000000.10101000.00000001.00000000

[*]A 1 means ignore, and a 0 means match

Using the information in Table 25-1, the ACL must match the range 192.168.1.0 to 192.168.1.255.

Do not look for a relationship between wildcard masks and subnet masks; wildcard masks serve an entirely different function from subnet masks. A wildcard mask is not the opposite of a subnet mask and serves an entirely different function. *Always consider a wildcard mask in binary form.* The wildcard mask 0.0.0.0 states that the ACL should match the entire host. 0.0.0.0 can also be represented by the term *any* or *host* in an ACL.

11.2.1–11.2.3—When you create an ACL, you need to choose to make a standard, extended, or named ACL. The following key points about each should help you choose wisely:

- **Standard**—This type of ACL uses the number range 1 to 99 and checks only the source address—that is, who is sending the packet.

- **Extended**—With an extended ACL, you can check the source, destination, protocol, and port. Extended ACLs use the number range 100 to 199.

- **Named**—Named ACLs do not use a range of numbers because the name is the identifier. Named ACLs can be configured as standard or extended ACLs. Named ACLs can be altered without deleting the entire ACL and recreating it, but you can add statements only to the end of a named ACL.

11.2.4—You should put an extended ACL as close to the source of the traffic you are filtering as possible. This allows the extended ACL to filter the traffic by looking at where it is headed (that is, by looking at the destination address). You should put a standard ACL as close to the destination of the traffic you are filtering as possible. A standard ACL cannot look at where the packet is going, but it can look at who sent it.

Summary

Today you reviewed how a network can control the flow of data at Layer 2 with CSMA/CD and at Layer 3 with ACLs and wildcard masks. You will review ACL theory and configuration on Days 19, 10, and 3. In the meantime, ponder this question: Should ACLs give you more control over a network or lessen the need to control a network? Taking a Networking Academy CCNA curriculum practice test will help you make this assessment. You may also want to read through pages 456–467 in the *CCNA Flash Cards and Exam Practice Pack* (CCNA Self-Study, exam #640-801), Second Edition (ISBN: 1587200791).

Your Notes

Evaluate Key Characteristics of WANs

A WAN connection allows you to link office, school, or private LANs across a large distance. Today you quickly review WANs, WAN protocols, and WAN connections and then further explore WAN characteristics on Day 18, "Choose WAN Services to Meet Customer Requirements." Module 2 from CCNA 1, Module 1 from CCNA 2, and Modules 2, 3, 4, and 5 from CCNA 4 discuss the key characteristics of WANs.

CCNA 1, Module 2

2.1.7—WANs operate over a large, geographically separated area. You can connect to a WAN using a modem, Integrated Service Digital Network (ISDN), digital subscriber line (DSL), Frame Relay, Synchronous Optical Network (SONET), T1, E1, T3, or E3. WANs often provide access over serial interfaces at lower speeds than a LAN.

CCNA 2, Module 1

1.1.1, 1.1.3, and 1.1.4—When you design a WAN, you will almost always coordinate with a communication service provider such as a local phone company. Routers, modems, and communication servers play an important role in WAN design, and routers often act as a gateway from your LAN to a WAN. The connections and protocols specific to a WAN operate at OSI Layers 1 and 2. These physical and data-link standards and protocols are different for a WAN than for a LAN.

1.2.7—Imagine that your box of connectivity equipment has just arrived in the mail and it is time to connect to the WAN. The phone company will ask you to connect your router, which can also be referred to as customer premises equipment (CPE) and the data terminal equipment (DTE). Your DTE will likely connect through a CSU/DSU (could be a modem) as the provider's data circuit-terminating equipment (DCE), and the provider will set the clocking with the DCE.

CCNA 4, Module 2

2.1.1 and 2.1.2—In CCNA 2 Module 1.2.7, you connected to the WAN and can now surf happily. You now need to be familiar with a few new WAN connectivity terms. You should know that you are connected to the provider's nearest exchange, or *central office (CO)*. The cabling between you and the CO is often called the *local loop* or *last mile*. The port in your building that the phone company installed is called the *demarcation point*. A common physical connection type for a DCE/DTE interface is a *High-Speed Serial Interface (HSSI)*. WAN connection speeds can range from bits per second to gigabits per second in full duplex. Your HSSI connects to a CSU/DSU to provide proper transmission of the signals over the link. A modem can also serve this purpose by modulating and then demodulating the signal in order to pass digital information over an analog line.

2.1.3—Table 24-1 displays the physical layer and data link layer standards for a WAN.

Table 24-1   WAN Physical and Data Link Layer Standards

Physical			Data Link
EIA/TIA-232	64 kbps	Point-to-point	Cisco HDLC, PPP, LAPB
EIA/TIA-449/530	Up to 2 Mbps	Packet switched	X.25, Frame Relay
EIA/TIA-612/613	HSSI up to 52 Mbps	Circuit switched	ISDN
V.35	48 kbps		
X.21	Synchronous digital		

2.1.4—A WAN connection uses a Layer 2 frame to encapsulate data. The most common WAN encapsulation uses the HDLC standard. An HDLC frame starts and ends with a flag field. Following the starting flag field is a header field that includes the address, control, and protocol field. A data field and FCS field follow, and the frame ends with a flag field. The control field identifies one of the following three types of frames:

- **Unnumbered frame**—This frame is for line setup messages.

- **Information frame**—This frame holds data.

- **Supervisory frame**—This frame controls data frame flow and can request retransmission if an error occurs.

PPP and Cisco HDLC have an extra field that identifies the network layer of the encapsulated data.

2.1.5—When you make a phone call, the exchange of the local carrier switches circuits to create a continuous circuit between you and the person you are calling. The phone system is considered a circuit-switched system. A phone call requires continuous connectivity, but a person who surfs the Web only needs to connect in short bursts to get and receive new information. For data communication, it is possible for many computers to share a connection and take turns requesting and receiving data as packets. A connection that shares capacity by switching packets for many nodes is called a *packet-switched network (PSN)*. The Internet is an example of a connectionless PSN where each packet contains full addressing information. Frame Relay is an example of a Layer 2 WAN connection-oriented PSN where the route is determined by switches and each frame carries an identifier called a data-link connection identifier (DLCI). Frame Relay switches create a virtual circuit (VC) between communicating hosts that exists only when the frame is being transferred. You can refer to a temporary virtual circuit as a switched virtual circuit (SVC). When a virtual circuit needs to exist forever, it is called a permanent virtual circuit (PVC).

2.1.6—To connect to a WAN, you can use a dedicated circuit and buy a fractional T1/E1 through T3/E3 or DSL or you can instead choose a switched circuit as one of the following:

- Circuit switched in the form of ISDN or the plain old telephone service (POTS)

- Packet switched in the form of X.25 or Frame Relay

- Cell switched as Asynchronous Transfer Mode (ATM)

If you choose packet switching and if your bandwidth requirements are low, you can save money if you request an SVC instead of a PVC. With an SVC, the provider can allow you to share a physical link with other subscribers.

CCNA 4, Module 3

3.1.1 and 3.1.4—WAN serial communication requires that frames are sent one bit at a time over the wire. Serial communication standards include RS-232-E, V.35, and HSSI. We will cover more of these terms on Day 18. As mentioned in "CCNA 2, Module 1" under 1.2.7, your router is the DTE and the provider allows you to connect to the DCE. Both a modem and a CSU/DSU can function as DCEs and are the entrance point to the service provider network. Modems auto-sense the clocking from the service provider line. A CSU/DSU typically is defaulted to auto sense it from the line, but may need to be configured. Your DTE connection to the CSU/DSU will be through a serial connection using one of the following standards: EIA/TIA-232, EIA/TIA-449, V.35, X.21, and EIA/TIA-530.

CCNA 4, Module 4

4.1.1—Local carriers use ISDN to provide a digital connection on the local loop for a subscriber. This digital connection allows you to exceed the 56 kbps bandwidth barrier of an analog connection. ISDN bearer (B) channels carry data at 64 kbps for each channel. The ISDN delta (D) channel is used to set up the call and for signaling. The call with ISDN is faster than a modem, and the ISDN connection allows for a PPP-encapsulated link.

4.3.1—Interesting traffic could be defined in many ways, but in the context of dial-on-demand routing (DDR) interesting traffic is network activity that causes a router to connect to a network. You can define a dialer-list on a Cisco router that tells the router what traffic should cause it to bring up a DDR link. A router that is set up for DDR will receive packets and first check to see if the packets should be forwarded to the DDR link, and if so, check to see if they meet the criteria for interesting traffic. If the packets fulfill both conditions, the router sets up the call and all traffic will be sent over the link until no more interesting traffic is sent and the idle timer timeout period completes.

CCNA 4, Module 5

5.1.1—If you were asked to name one packet-switched, connection-oriented, HDLC encapsulating, data link layer WAN technology, Frame Relay would be a good choice. Frame Relay switches act as a DCE for a router. Once the frame is forwarded from the DTE router to a Frame Relay switch, the network of Frame Relay switches moves the data to its destination. Usually you subscribe to a network of trunked Frame Relay switches owned by a public carrier.

5.1.2—You want to connect LAN1 to LAN2 across town using Frame Relay. First you call the phone company and connect your LAN1 router to their nearest Frame Relay switch. Your LAN1 router will have a unique DLCI that identifies it on the Frame Relay switch network. You then connect the LAN2 router to a nearby Frame Relay switch on the same phone company network. LAN2 will also have a DLCI that identifies it on the Frame Relay network. The phone company uses its Frame Relay switches to then establish a packet-switched PVC across town for your two LANs. The routers on LAN1 and LAN2 operate as Frame Relay access devices (FRADs).

Summary

Today you reviewed a comprehensive definition for a WAN, including its relation to the OSI model, and types of WAN connections. You learn more about these key WAN characteristics on Day 18. If you have *CCNA Flash Cards and Exam Practice Pack* (CCNA Self-Study, exam #640-801), Second Edition, look over pages 488–510.

Your Notes

Part II

23–18 Days Before the Exam— Planning and Design

Design a Simple LAN Using Cisco Technology

Previous days and topics about LANs spill together into LAN design with an additional focus on the Cisco three-layer hierarchical model. Important sections of the Cisco Networking Academy curriculum that cover LAN design are Modules 2, 5, 8, 9, and 10 from CCNA 1, Module 1 from CCNA 2, and Module 5 from CCNA 3.

CCNA 1, Module 2

2.1.3—Networks contain two main types of devices. End-user devices (computers, printers, and so on) and network devices (cables, hubs, and so on). Key network devices that glue a LAN together include the following:

- **Network interface card (NIC)**—Connects the host to a network and contains a MAC address
- **Repeaters**—Simply regenerate the signal
- **Active hubs**—Regenerate the signal and have multiple ports
- **Bridges**—Two ports that maintain a MAC address table for hosts
- **Switch**—Multiple ports that maintain a MAC address table for connected hosts
- **Routers**—Connects a LAN to a WAN

2.1.4—The terms to describe the physical topology of a network help you to explain how all of the devices are actually connected. These terms include the following:

- **Bus**—All devices connected to one arterial cable
- **Ring**—Each host connected to two other hosts forming a ring
- **Star**—All hosts connected to a hub or switch
- **Extended star**—Hosts connected to a hub or switch that is in turn connected to a hub or switch
- **Hierarchical**—Hosts connected to a hub or switch that is connected to another host or switch forming an extended star that is then connected to a proxy that handles traffic
- **Mesh**—A direct physical link from each host to every other host

2.1.5 and 2.1.6—Networks need a set of rules to determine how they communicate. These rules are defined as *protocols*. Network protocols control the type of connection, how data is transferred, and how to handle errors. Computers, NICs, peripheral devices, networking media, and network devices make up the main parts of a LAN. The most common LAN technologies are Ethernet, Token Ring, and FDDI.

CCNA 1, Module 5

5.1.1—The physical layer of a LAN focuses on the media (actual cables and technology) used to connect the machines and send information. Common technologies include Token Ring, FDDI, and Ethernet. The IEEE specifications for Ethernet are 802.3 for 10 Mbps, 802.3u for 100 Mbps, and 802.3z for 1000 Mbps. Category 5 unshielded twisted pair (UTP) carries most LAN signals today, but signals can be transmitted through coaxial cable, optical fiber, and wireless as well.

5.1.2—Ethernet was first implemented by Digital, Intel, and Xerox (DIX). Typically, Ethernet is implemented at the 100 Mbps (Fast Ethernet) level with Gigabit Ethernet as a backbone solution. This will change as the cost to implement Gigabit Ethernet drops.

5.1.3—Details about the type of Ethernet implementation can be deciphered from the TIA/EIA standards. 10Base5 implementations are 10 Mbps, baseband, and have a maximum length of 500 meters over coaxial cable. 1000BaseT implementations are 1000 Mbps, baseband, and use twisted pair (100 meter limit) as the media for transmission.

5.1.5— At the end of an Ethernet cable is the RJ-45 connector. This EIA/TIA-specified, eight-wire, clip-sporting piece of plastic comes in two flavors: T568A and T568B. If both ends of the cable are wired the same, both A or both B, you have a straight-through cable. You can use this kind of cable to connect a switch or hub to a router, a switch to a PC, or a hub to a PC. If you wire A on one end and B on the other end (or vice versa), you have created a crossover cable. This kind of cable allows you to connect a switch to a switch, a switch to a hub, a hub to a hub, a router to a router, a PC to a PC, or a router to a PC. Many newer devices, however, are auto-sensing and therefore allow use of a straight-through cable where you once needed a crossover. Save that crossover for your old stuff.

5.1.6—A repeater strengthens a signal to allow for greater cable and network distances. If you are going to extend your LAN to its absolute maximum, be sure to follow the 5-4-3-2-1 rule. A network can only have five (5) segments connected with four (4) Layer 1 and Layer 2 devices, only three (3) of those segments can have hosts attached, and two (2) of the segments have no hosts on one (1) big collision domain.

5.1.7—Repeaters have just two ports and serve the purpose of doubling the length of a cable. A hub is a multiport repeater. Cost used to be a primary factor when deciding between a hub and switch, but because the price of switches has decreased, cost is no longer an issue. A hub does little beyond concentrate the cables in a LAN to a central point. All devices are still in the same collision domain. Any group of devices that can cause a collision by attempting to communicate at the same time is in the same collision domain.

5.1.8—LANs can be connected using wireless signals. Improperly set up wireless LANs (WLANs) can have security risks. WLANs are predominately connected using radio frequency (RF) to communicate between transceivers (devices that have both a transmitter and a receiver). Because all networking devices see all signals, the WLAN is in one collision domain (similar to a hub).

5.1.9—Bridges move beyond that barrier of simple, senseless signal sending. A bridge can learn the MAC address of network hosts and determine whether or not to pass the signal to the separate segment. Bridges have only two ports.

5.1.10—A switch is able to learn the MAC address like a bridge, but a switch has many ports. Switches are able to create virtual circuits between devices that wish to communicate, so each port on a switch is its own collision domain. Switches communicate with each other to prevent loops. Configuration options in the software of a switch allow for the creation of virtual LANs, or the ability to divide switch ports into their own segment.

5.1.11—The network interface card (NIC) connects the host to a network. The MAC address that switches, bridges, and routers use to identify LAN hosts is burned on the NIC. The NIC is considered a Layer 2 device because it carries the MAC. Although routers identify hosts on a LAN using the MAC address, a router uses the host's Layer 3 IP address to forward data between networks.

5.1.12—Peer-to-peer networks (ten or fewer computers) allow users to control access and resources individually. Each computer acts as a server and client, allowing access to its resources while accessing other peer resources. File and print sharing are the common configurations on a peer-to-peer network. When the number of hosts exceeds ten, it is wise to implement a server and centralize access to resources for security and organizational purposes. The best and most adventurous way to learn this advice is through practical experience.

5.1.13— Using the client/server model in large networks makes sense because a central server can control host authentication, file and print access, and back up all vital network data. Servers provide a central point of failure, so an expert administrator and/or patient users prove necessary for the implementation of a server/client network.

CCNA 1, Module 8

8.1.1 and 8.1.2—A bridge initially does not know any MAC addresses on either of its segments. In order to begin filtering, a bridge listens to traffic on both of its ports and builds a table that associates MAC addresses with ports. Once all or many of the devices have communicated over the network, the bridge can determine whether or not to forward traffic between segments. A switch works like a bridge with many ports, and each port on a switch is its own collision domain or microsegment.

8.1.3—Switches can learn the source and destination of traffic and create a virtual circuit between two hosts on a network. This virtual circuit can then operate in full duplex and double the bandwidth. Switches also use content addressable memory (CAM) to quickly store and retrieve MAC table information and application-specific integrated circuits (ASICs) to speed up the process of filtering and forwarding traffic.

8.1.4—It takes time for a signal to travel across the media. This delay on a network is defined as *latency*. Outside of the speed limitations of the signal, switches cause delay when they wait to learn a destination MAC address, use circuits to process the signal, and use software to determine where to forward traffic.

8.2.1— When many devices use the same medium, they cannot send data at the same time or a collision will occur. The potential for collisions increases with the increase in hosts. To extend a network with a repeater or hub increases the potential for collisions. Point-to-point connections connect only two devices. An example of a point-to-point connection is a WAN link using a modem.

8.2.2—If you can increase collision domains on a network, then you can improve network performance. Imagine a LAN party with 50 hosts connected with hubs. In a single collision domain, only one host could communicate at a time. Each time two hosts attempted to communicate, a collision would occur and all hosts would be required to back off for a set amount of time. This kind of performance might have been okay for network games in the early '90s, but not so for the demands of today's serious LAN clan. It is important to follow the 5-4-3-2-1 rule described previously in the section "CCNA 1, Module 5" under 5.1.6 in order for a network (and network games) to function properly without excessive delay.

8.2.3—And how does one increase collision domains? Through segmentation with switches and routers. Switches filter traffic by MAC address and keep local traffic local. Routers operate at Layer 3 to forward data using the IP address, but routers also look at frames and drop any frames that do not have their destination MAC address.

8.2.4—When a host needs to locate another host, it initially broadcasts a request for that host's MAC address. This is called an Address Resolution Protocol (ARP) request. An ARP request is one example of a Layer 2 broadcast. Broadcasts pass across all switches using the broadcast address 0xFFFFFFFFFFFF. All hosts must process and respond to this request.

8.2.5—To prevent ARP requests from broadcasting to all devices on a network every time a host needs to resolve an address, you use a router. Routers use IP addresses and MAC addresses to filter and direct traffic. Routers are able to determine whether Layer 2 MAC broadcast traffic is destined for a host outside the LAN by looking at the IP address. If the IP of the destination host is outside the LAN, the router will respond in order to receive and forward the traffic. Switches can filter traffic destined for individual hosts and divide collision domains, and routers can filter broadcasts and divide broadcast domains.

CCNA 1, Module 9

9.2.1—NICs provide a host with a MAC address and the ability to express a unique identity to local switches, routers, and other network devices for Layer 2 traffic purposes. LANs are also designed to communicate with other LANs through routers, so a flat MAC addressing scheme is inferior to a hierarchical scheme using TCP/IP. IP addresses allow hosts to identify themselves by network and local location with a 32-bit address. The 32 ones and zeros in an IP address are divided into octets and represented in dotted decimal notation.

9.2.3—Hosts on a LAN with duplicate IP addresses cannot communicate. Each host must have the same network address and a unique host address. Each octet can only be a decimal number between 0 and 255.

9.2.4—For the purpose of designing a LAN, you just need general knowledge about address classes and how to implement them. Class A addresses use the first octet for the network ID and the last three octets to identify the hosts. Class B addresses use the first two octets to identify the network and the last two to identify the hosts. Class C addresses use the first three octets to identify the network and the last octet to identify the host. Class D addresses are reserved for multicasts, and Class E addresses are reserved for research. For LANs, a Class C addressing scheme often works well because you do not need more than 255 hosts. An example of how you might address a LAN with 3 hosts using a Class C addressing scheme is

- Host 1 is 192.168.1.2

- Host 2 is 192.168.1.3

- Host 3 is 192.168.1.4

Notice how the first three network octets remain the same for the entire network and the last octet, or host octet, identifies the host.

9.2.5—Many addresses are reserved for use outside of host identification. The first address (all zeros in the host section) on a network is reserved for the network, and the last address (all ones in the host section) is reserved for broadcasts.

9.2.6—RFC 1918 states that there are reserved Class A, B, and C address ranges for private LANs. The private ranges are as follows:

- Class A: 10.0.0.0 to 10.255.255.255

- Class B: 172.16.0.0 to 172.31.255.255

- Class C: 192.168.0.0 to 192.168.255.255

9.3.1—A host on a network can obtain an IP address automatically, or an administrator can statically assign the address. If two interfaces connected to a network are assigned the same IP address, this could cause conflicts and render both connected interfaces unable to communicate.

9.3.2—Some network administrators of small networks manually provide all hosts with static addresses. You will likely know when this type of administration does not fit your situation. It is a good idea to assign static addresses to network devices that other hosts must find on a regular basis, such as routers, servers, and network printers.

9.3.5—Dynamic Host Configuration Protocol (DHCP) is the most common way to allow hosts to obtain IP addresses automatically. Once an administrator sets up a DHCP server and identifies a range of available IP addresses, the hosts on the network can use DHCP to obtain an address.

CCNA 1, Module 10

10.2.2—Switches operate on the LAN to uniquely identify local machines by MAC address and regulate traffic between these hosts. If a host tries to communicate with a machine that is not on the LAN, the switch will search for that machine locally and find no matching MAC address. At this point, the router steps in and responds for that otherwise unreachable host. The switch forwards the traffic for that host to the router, and it is up to the router to use the IP address to find the host. A router operates mainly at Layer 3, and a switch operates at Layer 2.

CCNA 2, Module 1

1.1.3 and 1.2.6—The router is the connecting point for a LAN to other LANs or a WAN. A router is most commonly connected to a LAN on its Ethernet or Fast Ethernet interface. The router connects through a straight-through cable to a hub or switch.

CCNA 3, Module 5

5.1.1—When you design a LAN, keep the following four goals in mind:

- **Functionality**–The LAN has to allow users to accomplish their intended tasks.

- **Scalability**–The LAN should support growth without a need to make any major changes.

- **Adaptability**–The LAN should have the ability to upgrade to accommodate future technologies.

- **Manageability**–You should be able monitor and maintain the network in order to keep a stable environment.

5.1.2—If your network includes enterprise servers, place them in the main wiring closet, or main distribution facility (MDF). If your network also includes workgroup servers, you can place them in the intermediate distribution facility (IDF). Use switches to segment collision domains and routers to filter broadcasts.

5.1.3—Actions that you can perform while designing a LAN are as follows:

- **Gather LAN requirements and expectations**—Determine the skill level and attitude of the users as well as the demands put on the network by host hardware and software. Also document the financial and managerial structure of the network. Find out quickly who can make decisions and spend money and what they want.

- **Analyze the data you have gathered**—Use data from the previous action to estimate costs and a timeline to implement the project.

- **Design OSI Layers 1, 2, and 3 of the LAN**—Provide a well-organized chart of the network, data link, and physical layers of the LAN that can act as a road map for implementation. At the network and data link layers, include the logical topology and an addressing scheme to define the flow of the network. At the physical layer, create a cut sheet to define location and installation of devices in the facility.

5.1.4—To design the OSI Layer 1 scheme for a simple LAN, the use of fiber optics and Fast Ethernet is most common. Starting with a router connected to switches in your MDF, you can connect the switches to a patch panel and patch cables as horizontal cross-connects (HCCs) to the hosts. If your building exceeds the 100-meter limit for Category 5 UTP to reach all hosts, you can use fiber optics as the backbone vertical cross-connects (VCCs) to IDFs and then distribute connections. From the IDFs, you can use 10/100BaseTX, Category 5e UTP to connect from these wiring closets to the hosts. This structure can follow the TIA/EIA-568-A standards including your wiring scheme.

5.1.5—Your OSI Layer 2 design will focus on how the LAN will forward frames. To microsegment collision domains, you should use switches. HCCs are direct to hosts and should balance with a faster VCC between wiring closets. Once you have determined how many ports you will need for all hosts and connections to the LAN, you can place appropriate switches in the MDF and IDFs. Switch ports have only two hosts per collision domain with a source and destination host. The use of hubs instead of switches increases the size of collision domains to all hosts connected and affects bandwidth.

5.1.6—Layer 3 LAN design centers around the placement and configuration of routers on the LAN. Routers commonly forward data based on IP addressing, connect LANs, and divide broadcast domains between the LANs. Routers can also act as firewalls and provide a WAN connection. You can divide Layer 2 switches into virtual LANs (VLANs) to separate networks at Layer 3, but you need a router to communicate between VLANs.

5.2.1—At this point, you need to switch gears and focus on the Cisco Three-Layer Hierarchical Model. This model consists of the core, distribution, and access layers, which provide an outline for the types of devices and connectivity necessary in a large network. The core layer serves as the backbone reserved for high-speed transmission. The distribution layer divides the core layer from the access layer with policy. The access layer connects users and remote sites to the network. Collision domain microsegmentation and MAC address filtering also occur at the access layer.

5.2.2—Access layer switches operate at Layer 2 of the OSI model, provide microsegmentation, and can be separated into VLANs. You could use Catalyst 1900, 2820, 2950, 4000, and 5000 series switches at the access layer.

5.2.3 and 5.2.4—The distribution layer handles packets and OSI Layer 3 policies so that the core layer remains fast and efficient. Distribution layer devices include OSI Layer 2 and Layer 3 switches. VLANs, ACLs, and aggregation in the wiring closet at the distribution layer protect the core layer from handling these functions. You could use Catalyst 2926G, 3550, 3560, 5000, and 6000 families at the distribution layer.

5.2.5—As the backbone of the network, the core layer is designed to move packets as quickly as possible. Redundant paths implemented with Ethernet or ATM characterize the core layer. No access list implementation or packet manipulation occurs at the core layer. You need a beefy OSI Layer 2 or 3 switch to handle the demands of the core layer, and the Catalyst 6500, 8500, IGX 8400, and Lightstream 1010 fit the bill.

Summary

Networking devices, logical structure, and design layers surface any time you design, explain, or document a LAN. These concepts also show up often on the CCNA. Browse through pages 13–66 of the *CCNA Flash Cards and Exam Practice Pack* (CCNA Self-Study, exam #640-801), Second Edition, if you have time.

Your Notes

Design an IP Addressing Scheme to Meet Design Requirements

Day 27, "Evaluate the TCP/IP Communication Process and Its Associated Protocols," discussed basic IP addressing, and today you learn the topics that allow you to be flexible and creative with IP addressing design. It is important to chop away at subnets and use advanced addressing to design a more efficient and secure network. You will cover a quick review of the topics from Modules 1 and 9 from CCNA 1 and then learn new concepts in Module 10 from CCNA 1 and Module 1 from both CCNA 3 and CCNA 4.

CCNA 1, Module 1

1.2.5–1.2.7—You cannot leave out binary in the quest to understand IP addressing. Table 22-1 shows the powers of 2 for an 8-bit binary number, and Table 22-2 shows an example of an IP address in both dotted decimal and 32-bit binary. Notice that the IP address is made up of four sets of 8 bits (octets). If you are not sure how this conversion works, refer to Day 27.

Table 22-1   One Octet of an IP Address

Bits and Powers of 2	Decimal Equivalent
1 1 1 1 1 1 1 1 128 64 32 16 8 4 2 1	128+64+32+16+8+4+2+1 = 255

Table 22-2   Binary-to-Decimal Conversion for an IP Address

Numbering System	IP Address
Decimal	192.168.1.7
Binary	11000000.10101000.00000001.00000111

CCNA 1, Module 9

9.2.1–9.2.8—On Day 27 you covered default address classes and reserved, public, and private IP addresses. The main points necessary for today are outlined in Tables 22-3 through 22-5. Table 22-3 shows Class A, B, C, D, and E IP addresses.

Table 22-3   Class A, B, C, D, and E IP Addresses

Class	Binary Start	1st Octet Range	Network (N) and host (H) Octets	Number of Hosts	Bits in Network Address
Class A*	0	1–126	N.H.H.H	About 16 million	8
Class B	10	128–191	N.N.H.H	65,535	16
Class C	110	192–223	N.N.N.H	254	24
Class D	1110	224–239	H.H.H.H	Multicast	28
Class E	1111	240–255	RESEARCH	RESEARCH	RESEARCH

* The Class A address 127.0.0.0 is reserved for the loopback.

Table 22-4 shows an example of the addresses reserved on a network to represent the broadcast and the entire network.

Table 22-4   Reserved Network and Broadcast Address Example

Network Default Class C	Binary Host All 0s Network Address	Binary Host All 1s Broadcast Address	Useable Hosts
192.168.1.0	192.168.1.0	192.168.1.255	192.168.1.1 to 192.168.1.254

Table 22-5 lists the Class A, Class B, and Class C private address ranges, which are defined in the IETF RFC 1918.

Table 22-5   RFC 1918 Private Network Addresses

Class	Address Range
Class A	10.0.0.0 to 10.255.255.255
Class B	172.16.0.0 to 172.31.255.255
Class C	192.168.0.0 to 192.168.255.255

CCNA 1, Module 10

10.3.1 and 10.3.2—You can break up the Class A, B, and C default networks into smaller networks by identifying individual bits in the host portion as network bits. The term for this practice is *subnetting,* which allows you to efficiently use IP addresses, divide broadcast domains on your network, and add security with access lists.

10.3.3—A default Class C network has a subnet mask of 255.255.255.0. You have the entire last octet to address hosts (minus the network and broadcast address). If you borrow bits from the host portion, the subnet mask will reflect the bits that you have borrowed, and you will have more networks but fewer hosts for each network. Table 22-6 provides the bits borrowed from the host portion, the subnet mask in both decimal and slash format, and the amount of networks and hosts, and to subnet the last octet of a default Class C.

Table 22-6   Bits Borrowed and Corresponding Mask for a Class C Network

Bits Borrowed	1	2	3	4	5	6	7	8
Mask	128	192	224	240	248	252	254	255
Slash format	/25	/26	/27	/28	/29	/30	/31	/32
Total subnets	2*	4	8	16	32	64	N/A	N/A
Useable subnets*	0*	2*	6*	14*	30*	62*	N/A	N/A
Total hosts	128*	64	32	16	8	4	N/A	N/A
Usable hosts	126*	62	30	14	6	2	N/A	N/A

*Refers to CCNA 3, Module 1. The /25 subnet is now usable as well as the number of subnets listed in the total subnets row. RFC 1878 (Dec. 1995) started the use of all zeros and all ones for subnets. Make sure that you understand when you can use the all zeros and all ones subnets.

You can determine all of the information in Table 22-6 by using the binary representation and the powers of 2. As an example, the /26 network means that there are 26 bits total for the network portion. (Remember that a default Class C uses 24 bits.) You have borrowed 2 bits from the last octet and changed them from host bits (0) to network bits (1), so the last octet of the mask is the decimal representation of 11000000, or 192. To find the amount of networks, you can insert the number of bits borrowed into the formula 2^n-2 (unless you are using the all ones and all zeros subnets). In this case, your result is two networks available. If you look at the number of zeros in the mask 11000000, you can place those remaining bits in the formula 2^n-2 and you will find that you have 62 hosts available per network.

10.3.4—To continue with the example of 2 bits borrowed, you can also determine the interval for the subnetworks using the mask. In this case, you can use host bits available and apply the formula 2^n without subtracting 2. This gives you an interval of 64. Using this interval, you can start with the zero subnet and then add 64 to identify your networks. The host range would fall between the network and broadcast addresses. Table 22-7 provides an example of the networks and host ranges available for a default Class C network with 2 bits borrowed.

Table 22-7   Subnetworks for 192.168.1.0 with 2 Bits Borrowed (255.255.255.192 Mask)

Subnetwork Number	Subnetwork ID	Host Range	Broadcast ID
0	192.168.1.0	.1–.62	192.168.1.63
1	192.168.1.64	.63–.126	192.168.1.127
2	192.168.1.128	.129–.190	192.168.1.191
3	192.168.1.192	.193–.254	192.168.1.255

Remember that the subnetwork ID cannot be assigned to an interface. Use of the first and last subnets is discussed later today in the section "CCNA 3, Module 1."

10.3.5—You need to rely heavily on the use of binary representation and the 2^n-2 formula (unless you are using the zeros and ones subnets) when subnetting a Class A or Class B network.

It is technically the same as subnetting a Class C, but you may need to deal with higher powers of 2. Table 22-8 provides a subnetted Class B network as an example with the first four subnetworks. (There would be 128 total.)

Table 22-8   Subnetworks for 172.16.0.0 with 7 Bits Borrowed (255.255.254.0 Mask)

Subnetwork Number	Subnetwork ID	Host Range	Broadcast ID
0	172.16.0.0	.0.1–1.254	172.16.1.255
1	172.16.2.0	.2.1–3.254	172.16.3.255
2	172.16.4.0	.4.1–5.254	172.16.5.255
3	172.16.6.0	.6.1–7.254	172.16.7.255

10.3.6—As mentioned on Day 27, a router uses the AND operator to determine the network and host portion of an address. With subnetworks it is important that a router know the subnet mask for a network in order to forward the packet to the correct subnetwork. Table 22-9 reviews the ANDing process with an address from subnetwork 1 in Table 22-8.

Table 22-9   Using the AND Operator to Determine a Network Address

AND Operator	IP Address and Subnet Mask to Network Address
0 AND 0 = 0	IP address 172.16.2.38 Mask 255.255.254.0
0 AND 1 = 0	IP address 10101100.00010000.00000010.00100110
1 AND 0 = 0	Subnet mask 11111111.11111111.11111110.00000000
1 AND 1 = 1	Result 10101100.00010000.00000010.00000000
	Network address 172.16.2.0

CCNA 3, Module 1

1.1.1—You can efficiently use IP addresses by implementing variable-length subnet masks (VLSMs). Using VLSMs, you can choose the subnet mask that best suits the number of hosts for each section of the network. An example is to divide a Class C /24 mask to use the /30 mask for a point-to-point connection and then a /28 mask for a network with ten hosts. Static routes and only certain routing protocols such as Open Shortest Path First (OSPF), Integrated Intermediate System-to-Intermediate System (Intermediate IS-IS), Enhanced Interior Gateway Routing Protocol (EIGRP), and Routing Information Protocol version 2 (RIPv2) support VLSM.

1.1.2—As noted by the asterisks in Table 22-6, you can use the first and last subnets in conjunction with VLSM, so you do not need to subtract 2 to determine usable subnets. The **no ip subnet-zero** command enables use of these subnets in Cisco IOS software versions before Cisco IOS Release 12.0. After Cisco IOS Release 12.0, routers can use subnet zero by default.

1.1.3 and 1.1.4—Consider the three subnetworks in use in Table 22-10 applied to a network with a serial point-to-point connection between two routers with 250 host LANs connected to each router.

Table 22-10   Subnetworks for 172.16.0.0 with 8 Bits Borrowed (255.255.255.0 Mask)

Subnetwork Number	Subnetwork ID	Mask	Host Range	Broadcast ID
0	172.16.0.0	/24	0.1–0.254	172.16.0.255
1	172.16.1.0	/24	1.1–1.254	172.16.1.255
2	172.16.2.0	/24	2.1–2.254	172.16.2.255

Notice that the point-to-point link is flagrantly using 254 hosts when it only needs 2. You can free up most of those hosts by implementing VLSM and using the networks outlined in Table 22-11.

Table 22-11   Subnetworks for 172.16.0.0 with VLSMs

Subnetwork Number	Subnetwork ID	Mask	Host Range	Broadcast ID
0	172.16.0.4	/30	0.5–0.6	172.16.0.7
1	172.16.1.0	/24	1.1–1.254	172.16.1.255
2	172.16.2.0	/24	2.1–2.254	172.16.2.255

This configuration leaves many available subnetworks in the 172.16.0.0 space by using the /30 mask. Remember when you are using VLSM that your host ranges cannot overlap. Make sure that you do not later use a large subnetwork (an example would be 172.16.0.0 /24 for Table 22-11) that includes a small subnetwork you are already using. You can check host ranges for duplicates, but for complicated networks it might help to find a VLSM chart on the Internet and use it to cross out used subnetworks.

1.1.5—If you use VLSM and keep your subnets sequential or grouped together, a router can represent the group of subnets as one large subnet to other routers. This type of route aggregation, or summarization, keeps routing tables small between networks. VLSM and classless interdomain routing (CIDR) allow for more efficient use of IP address space and routing tables.

CCNA 4, Module 1

1.1.1–1.1.3—If you have designed a network using nonroutable private addresses (specified earlier in Table 22-5), you can still connect these internally addressed hosts to the Internet using network address translation (NAT) and port address translation (PAT). Using only NAT, you can represent an internal IP address as an external (real) IP address. If you have an internal PC hostA with an address of 10.0.0.5, your router has an interface on the Internet with the address 179.8.80, and hostA attempts to communicate with an Internet server with the address 128.23.2.2, the following could happen with NAT:

- HostA will send its packet with the *inside local address* of 10.0.0.5.

- The router will replace the source address 10.0.0.5 with its *inside global address* of 179.9.8.80 as the source address for the packet on the Internet.

- The router will send the packet to the Internet server's *outside global address* of 128.23.2.2.

- When the router receives a reply from the Internet server, it will look in its NAT table and see an entry that maps the packet from the server back to hostA's inside local address of 10.0.0.5.

NAT can only map one Internet IP address to one private IP address. A pool of Internet addresses can be dynamically mapped to private addresses, but the ratio is still one to one. Overloading, or assigning multiple private addresses to one Internet IP address, proves possible with NAT and PAT together. PAT uses source port addressing to represent multiple private addresses with one Internet IP address.

Summary

Now you should be able to design a network that incorporates NAT, PAT, VLSM, CIDR, RFC 1918, and good ol' IP. This knowledge not only puts your best foot forward at a job interview, but also helps you to understand and troubleshoot a number of OSI Layer 3 issues. Practice and research different methods and examples to help solidify your abilities with subnetting and VLSM. If you have the *CCNA Flash Cards and Exam Practice Pack* (CCNA Self-Study, exam #640-801), Second Edition, look over pages 141–146 and 475–480.

Your Notes

Select an Appropriate Routing Protocol Based on User Requirements

CCNA objectives for today and Day 28, "Evaluate the Characteristics of Routing Protocols," complement each other. Today you focus on comparing routing protocol features to perfect your ability to pick the proper protocol. If you have completed Day 28 and can characterize routing protocols, you should not have much trouble understanding the concepts behind the features. Today we first outline the function of a routing protocol with information from CCNA 1 Module 10. You will then review only the information that compares routing protocols from Module 6 of CCNA 2 and Modules 1, 2, and 3 from CCNA 3.

CCNA 1, Module 10

10.1.1—Routing protocols allow routers to learn about available networks. Routed protocols provide addresses for hosts to communicate over a network. As a routed protocol, IP uses a subnet mask to identify the network. Day 27 and Day 22 explained how a subnet mask allows a router to identify a group of IP addresses as a network.

10.2.1—Routing occurs at OSI Layer 3. Routers look only at an individual address in order to apply a netmask and then find the path to the network. Routers see networks, not individual addresses. The individual IP address becomes necessary only to determine the final destination of the packet. Other OSI Layer 3 routed protocols are Internetwork Packet Exchange (IPX) and AppleTalk. NetBEUI is the most common nonroutable protocol.

10.2.2 and 10.2.3—As a switched LAN grows, it becomes necessary to segment the LAN with routers. Routing and switching processes both forward data based on addressing, but switching occurs at Layer 2 using the MAC address. The MAC address is unique to the LAN and allows the switch to forward frames and maintain a flat table of MAC addresses without any specific organization. The router maintains a routing table of connected networks and uses the Layer 3 addressing scheme to forward packets outside of the LAN and to other LANs. The hierarchical nature of Layer 3 addresses allows the router to group and organize network knowledge. Additional examples of these Layer 3 routed protocols are Banyan VINES and Xerox Network Systems (XNS).

10.2.5–10.2.9—Day 28 presents most remaining information in Module 10 using summaries from CCNA 2 Module 7. CCNA 1 Module 10 does add that routers determine network paths using the following information from a routing table:

- **Protocol Type**—The Layer 3 routed protocol

- **Next-hop association**—The directly connected network or a network that the router has learned about through a routing protocol

- **Routing metric** —Used to determine the most efficient path

- **Outbound interfaces**—Which interface to forward the packet for the specified route

CCNA 2, Module 6

6.2.1–6.3.4—Table 21-1 and Table 21-2 review points about types of routing protocols covered in Day 28 from CCNA 2 Module 6 with the addition of administrative distances for each routing protocol.

Table 21-1 compares distance vector and link-state protocols.

Table 21-1   Distance Vector and Link-State Protocols

Distance Vector	Link-State
Routers send periodic updates of the entire routing table to neighbors.	Routers send link-state advertisements (LSAs) to update other routers only when there is a topology change.
Routers see only neighboring routers.	Routers use the LSAs to build a full loop-free topology of the network, but this requires more memory than a distance vector protocol.
Routers use a metric to determine the cost path for a route and build a routing table.	Routers use the Shortest Path First (SPF) algorithm and LSAs to build a shortest path tree as well as a routing table.

Table 21-2 describes specific distance vector, link-state, and hybrid protocols.

Table 21-2   Routing Protocols

Protocol Name	AD	Type	Description
Routing Information Protocol (RIP)	120	Interior distance vector	Broadcasts updates every 30 seconds and uses hop count as the metric with a maximum of 16
Interior Gateway Routing Protocol (IGRP)	100	Interior distance vector	Cisco proprietary protocol that broadcasts updates every 90 seconds and uses bandwidth, load, reliability, and delay as a metric
Open Shortest Path First (OSPF)	110	Interior link-state	Nonproprietary protocol that updates only when there is a change in topology. OSPF uses cost as a metric
Enhanced Interior Gateway Routing Protocol (EIGRP)	90	Interior hybrid	Cisco proprietary protocol that uses both link-state and distance vector features and multicasts updates on 224.0.0.10. EIGRP uses the same metrics as IGRP
Border Gateway Protocol (BGP)	20	Exterior distance vector	Used to route between autonomous systems

CCNA 3, Module 1

1.2.1–1.2.3—Table 21-3 compares RIPv1 and RIPv2.

Table 21-3   RIPv1 vs. RIPv2

RIPv1	RIPv2
Simple configuration.	Simple configuration.
Does not send subnet mask information in the routing update. All subnets must have the same subnet mask.	Sends subnet mask information with updates. Supports VLSM and CIDR.
No authentication.	Supports MD5 authentication.
Broadcasts updates over 255.255.255.255.	Sends updates as multicasts over 224.0.0.9.

CCNA 3, Module 2

2.1.1–2.1.6—The following points are additional features of a link-state protocol:

- Link-state protocols send hellos periodically to obtain information about neighboring routers.

- When a network changes, a router will flood LSAs on a specific multicast address across the specified network area.

- LSAs allow the router to create a topological database of the network, use the Dijkstra algorithm to determine the shortest path for each network, build the shortest path tree, and use the tree to build the routing table.

- Flooding LSAs across a network can affect overall bandwidth on a network and cause each router to recalculate a full topological database.

- A network using a link-state protocol must be broken up into small enough areas to maintain network efficiency and use routers with sufficient memory and processing power.

2.2.1–2.2.7 —OSPF includes these features:

- OSPF is a nonproprietary link-state protocol that allows you to control the flow of updates with areas.

- OSPF allows more than 15 maximum hops, and large networks can be divided into areas.

- OSPF areas communicate with a backbone area to reduce routing protocol traffic and routing table size.

- OSPF-enabled routers are true to their link-state definition in that they maintain a full loop-free topological database of the network.

- Each OSPF-enabled router maintains a unique adjacency database that tracks only neighbor routers.

- OSPF-enabled routers elect a designated router (DR) and backup designated router (BDR) as central points for routing updates.

- VLSM support, a bandwidth-based metric, a loop-free SPF tree, and rapid convergence through LSAs are key features of OSPF.

- OSPF routers that are connected on broadcast multiaccess networks such as fiber or Ethernet or nonbroadcast multiaccess networks such as Frame Relay elect a single router to handle updates called the DR. To avoid a single point of failure, they also elect a BDR.

- OSPF hello packets typical to link-state protocols go out over the multicast address 224.0.0.5. If the connection is broadcast or point-to-point, the hellos go out every 10 seconds; and if the connection is nonbroadcast multiaccess (NMBA), the packets go out every 30 seconds.

CCNA 3, Module 3

3.1.1 and 3.1.2—Each of the following points identifies an EIGRP feature:

- EIGRP and IGRP routing protocols can function seamlessly together on a network.

- EIGRP also supports VLSM where IGRP does not. A router running only IGRP will see EIGRP routes as IGRP routes.

- As an advanced distance vector routing protocol, EIGRP uses functions from both link-state and distance vector protocols.

- Like OSPF, EIGRP collects multiple databases of network information to build a routing table.

- EIGRP uses a neighboring table in the same way that OSPF uses an adjacency database to maintain information on adjacent routers.

- Unlike OSPF, EIGRP uses a distance vector diffusing update algorithm (DUAL) to recalculate a topology.

- EIGRP maintains a topology table that contains routes learned from all configured network protocols.

- The neighboring and topology table allow EIGRP to use DUAL to identify the best route, or the *successor route*, and enter it into the routing table. Backup routes, or *feasible successor* routes, are kept only in the topology table.

- In the topology table, EIGRP can also tag routes as internal or external. Internal routes are from inside the EIGRP AS, and external routes come from other routing protocols and outside the EIGRP AS.

3.1.3 and 3.1.4—Advanced features of EIGRP that set it apart from other distance vector routing protocols include:

- **Rapid convergence**—EIGRP uses the DUAL finite-state machine (FSM) to develop a full loop-free topology of the network allowing all routers to converge at the same time.

- **Efficient use of bandwidth**—EIGRP, like OSPF, sends out partial updates and hello packets, but these packets go only to routers that need the information. EIGRP also develops neighboring relationships with other routers.

- **Support for VLSM and CIDR**—EIGRP sends the subnet mask information allowing the network to be divided beyond default subnet masks.

- **Multiple network layer support**—Rather than rely on TCP/IP to send and receive updates, EIGRP uses Reliable Transport Protocol (RTP) as its own proprietary means of sending updates.

- **Independence from routed protocols**—EIGRP supports IP, IPX, and AppleTalk. EIGRP has a modular design that uses protocol-dependant modules (PDMs) to support other routing protocols, so changes to reflect revisions in the other protocols have to be made only to the PDM and not EIGRP.

Summary

Once you are comfortable with the key features and comparisons of each routing protocol, you will be able to factor network size, growth potential, Layer 3 addressing, and compatibility into your selection of the proper routing protocol. If you have read through pages 388–450 of the *CCNA Flash Cards and Exam Practice Pack* (CCNA Self-Study, exam #640-801), Second Edition, it should be very easy to RIP (pun intended) through them again. You can focus on the commands on a later day. Remember that you have both Day 28 and the curriculum as a reference for today.

Your Notes

Design a Simple Internetwork Using Cisco Technology

When you interconnect LANs, you create an internetwork. Once you step outside of the LAN, you will find storage-area networks (SANs), virtual private networks (VPNs), and metropolitan-area networks (MANs). Modules 2 and 8 from CCNA 1, Module 8 from CCNA 3, and Modules 1 and 2 from CCNA 4 teach the concepts you need to understand in order to define and design internetworks. You will cover specific WAN service technologies on Day 18, "Choose WAN Services to Meet Customer Requirements."

CCNA 1, Module 2

2.1.7–2.1.10—A LAN provides connectivity for local devices in the same room or building. Table 20-1 explains the advanced concepts behind networks that are more than just a LAN.

Table 20-1   Network Types

Network Type	Function
Wide-area network (WAN)	Connects LANs using serial transmission over a large geographic area to provide remote resources, e-mail, and the Internet.
Metropolitan-area network (MAN)	Connects LANs in a metropolitan area using private lines, a wireless bridge, or optical services.
Storage-area network (SAN)	Provides high-performance, fault-tolerant, scalable storage for servers over a separate network from the client/server network.
Virtual private network (VPN)	Provides a private network that exists inside of a public network. Clients connect through a secure tunnel to the VPN router at the destination.

2.1.11—Three main types of VPNs exist:

- **Access VPNs**—Allow a client from a home or small office to connect to the main site.

- **Intranet VPNs**—Provide a connection for regional and remote offices for employees.

- **Extranet VPNs**—Link business partners to an internal network. These partners do not have to be employees of the business.

2.1.12—On a LAN, you can configure a local intranet. This intranet provides employees using the LAN browser access to information and applications on a local server. If your LAN is connected to a WAN, you can provide extranet access to this server for Internet users with the proper authentication.

CCNA 1, Module 8

8.2.7—The term *segment* holds many meanings in networking. Segments are the OSI Layer 4 protocol data unit (PDU). A segment can represent a physical portion of a network divided by repeaters or a logical portion of a network divided by routers. Module 8 from CCNA 3 discusses how to segment a network logically with switches.

CCNA 3, Module 8

8.1.1 and 8.1.2—If you have one switch with 24 connected employees, then you have one large broadcast domain. Imagine that these 24 employees belong to three groups and you want to divide the LAN into three broadcast domains. To divide this network, you could buy two more switches, or you could use the capabilities of the switch to create VLANs. Switches capable of VLANs allow you to use software to logically divide the network into separate broadcast domains. When you divide a switch into VLANs, it performs the following actions:

- The switch maintains a separate MAC address table for each VLAN, and each VLAN is its own broadcast domain.

- The switch uses only the MAC address table from a specific VLAN to learn addresses and forward frames for that VLAN.

- The Layer 2 switch does not allow communication across VLANs without a Layer 3 router.

- The switch is capable of connecting to other switches and sharing VLAN information. A frame forwarded from VLAN1 on switchA will be seen by VLAN1 on switchB only if the switches are trunked. (Expect more about trunking on Day 14, "Configure a Switch with VLANs and Interswitch Communication.")

8.1.3–8.1.5—VLANs give you complete control over the logical topology of your network despite the physical arrangement your switches. You can use software to control VLAN membership by MAC address or logical address. This dynamic membership VLAN allows users to move around and remain in the same VLAN. If you do not want users to move around, you can create a static VLAN. To create a static, port-centric VLAN, you can map each port on a switch to a VLAN regardless of who connects to that port.

CCNA 4, Module 1

1.1.1–1.1.3—As discussed on Day 22, "Design an IP Addressing Scheme to Meet Design Requirements," your computer needs a registered IP address to communicate on the Internet, but you can use an RFC 1918 private address range with a LAN and implement network address translation (NAT) and port address translation (PAT) on your router to connect your entire LAN to the Internet with just one outside IP address. Millions of cable Internet and digital subscriber line (DSL) subscribers have routers that can implement NAT and PAT.

1.2.1 and 1.2.2—If you design a LAN connected to the Internet using NAT and PAT, it would be a great idea to add Dynamic Host Configuration Protocol (DHCP). DHCP provides a way for any host that you connect to the LAN to automatically obtain an IP address from your router using the transport layer User Datagram Protocol (UDP) ports 67 and 68. DHCP replaced the Bootstrap Protocol (BOOTP) as a more advanced means of allocating an IP address. BOOTP requires you to configure a static map of IP addresses for each client you add to the network. DHCP can lease an IP address to a client from a pool of addresses and provide other configuration information such as a domain name.

1.2.3—DHCP offers three types of IP address allocation:

- Automatic allocation of a permanent address

- Manual allocation of an address configured by the administrator

- Dynamic allocation of an address leased for a limited period of time

You can configure the DHCP pool to include any range of addresses from one subnet. Configuration parameters you can set for the host in DHCP include the following:

- Subnet mask

- Gateway router

- Domain name

- Domain name server

- Windows Internet naming WINS server

1.2.4—To obtain an IP address using DHCP, a client first sends a DHCPDISCOVER broadcast. A DHCP server will either respond to the broadcast with a unicast DHCPOFFER or forward the request to another DHCP server. A Cisco DCHP server will ping its address pool twice, by default, to check for used IP addresses before sending a DHCPOFFER. The DHCPOFFER can include an IP address, DNS server, and lease time. If the client receives DHCPOFFERs from more than one DHCP server, it will typically accept the first offer it receives. The client notifies the network that it has accepted a request by broadcasting a DHCPREQUEST with the accepted configuration. The DHCP server will then send a DHCPACK unicast, and the client can start using the IP address. If the client detects that an IP address is in use on the network, it will send a DHCPDECLINE and start another request. When the client is done with the IP address, it will send a DHCPRELEASE.

CCNA 4, Module 2

2.3.1 and 2.3.2—When you design the WAN portion of an internetwork, consider the following factors:

- You will likely purchase your WAN connections from a communications provider for cost and legal reasons.

- You must balance the cost of WAN connections with the speed necessary for your WAN to function. WAN connections are slower than LAN connections but may need to support voice and video as well as data.

- WANs function at the lower three layers of the OSI model but focus on Layers 1 and 2.

To design a WAN, consider the following steps:

Step 1   Locate LANS.

Step 2   Analyze traffic.

Step 3   Plan a topology.

Step 4   Plan bandwidth.

Step 5   Choose technology.

Step 6   Evaluate cost.

Summary

At the point that you plan to segment LANs and connect them with WAN technologies, you begin the process to create an entire internetwork. When you study the specific WAN technologies on Day 18, you will be ready to move on to the even more exciting sections about configuration and troubleshooting. In your notes, it might help to diagram the DHCP process and key features of VLANs. Before turning the page, you might like to quickly look at pages 59–68 and 350–354 in the *CCNA Flash Cards and Exam Practice Pack* (CCNA Self-Study, exam #640-801), Second Edition.

Your Notes

Develop an Access List to Meet User Specifications

Today you review the guidelines for creating an access control list (ACL), which is covered in CCNA 2, Module 11. Short days like today provide a great opportunity to take a Cisco Academy online practice CCNA test or get a head start on the next day.

CCNA 2, Module 11

11.1.1–11.1.3—Remember the following guidelines for an ACL from Day 25, "Evaluate Rules for Packet Control":

- The way to revise an ACL is to delete and re-create it unless it is a named ACL.

- A router checks ACL statements in the order in which you create them.

- A router stops checking ACL statements after the first match.

- At the end of every ACL, there is an implicit deny.

- You can apply one ACL per protocol per direction per interface.

- Place *extended* ACLs closest to the *source*.

- Place *standard* ACLs closest to the *destination*.

- An ACL should filter specific addresses first and then groups of addresses.

- Do not work with an access list that is applied.

- When an IP ACL rejects a packet, it sends an ICMP implicit deny.

- Outbound ACLs do not affect traffic originating from the router.

To control traffic with an ACL, you first create the ACL and then apply the ACL in a direction to a port. To create the ACL, you use the command **access-list** in global configuration mode. To apply the ACL, you switch to interface mode and use the command **ip access-group**. Both commands have syntax and parameters that will be covered with examples on Day 10, "Implement an Access List." When you identify a group of IP addresses in an ACL, you use the wildcard mask to specify the range.

11.1.4—Do not look for a relationship between wildcard masks and subnet masks; wildcard masks serve an entirely different function from subnet masks. As explained on Day 25, the IP address 192.168.1.7 with the wildcard mask 0.0.0.255 tells the router that the ACL must match the range 192.168.1.0 to 192.168.1.255. A wildcard mask uses binary ANDing to show what part of an IP address should be matched. The wildcard mask 0.0.0.0 states that the ACL should match the entire host. 0.0.0.0 can also be represented by the term **any** or **host** in an ACL.

11.1.5—After you have created and applied an ACL, you can verify that it is present by looking at the configuration or by looking at the specific interface where you applied the ACL. On Day 3, "Troubleshoot an Access List," you will cover the commands and output associated with ACL verification.

11.2.1–11.2.3—Remember the following key points about each type of ACL:

- **Standard ACL**—This type of ACL uses the number range 1 to 99 and checks only the source address, or who is sending the packet.

- **Extended ACL**—With an extended ACL, you can check the source, destination, protocol, and port. Extended ACLs use the number range 100 to 199.

- **Named ACL**—Named ACLs do not use a range of numbers because the name is the identifier. Named ACLs can be configured as standard or extended ACLs.

11.2.4—You should put an extended ACL as close to the source of the traffic you are filtering as possible, because an extended ACL is able to look at the destination address in a packet. You should put a standard ACL as close to the destination of the traffic you are filtering as possible because a standard ACL looks only at the source address of a packet.

11.2.5—ACLs allow you to control traffic, but more importantly they also allow you to protect users. Border routers configured with ACLs can act as firewalls and protect internal LANs from attacks that originate from outside your network.

11.2.6—A router has five virtual ports called VTY lines that you can control with an ACL. You should apply the same restrictions to all VTY lines on a router and use only numbered ACLs.

Summary

First you determine the traffic that you want to permit and deny, and then you create the rules in the list, and lastly you apply the ACL to an interface. The implementation guidelines outlined today prepare you for ACL configuration and troubleshooting on days 10 and 3. If you have a copy of *CCNA Flash Cards and Exam Practice Pack* (CCNA Self-Study, exam #640-801), Second Edition, look through pages 456–468.

Your Notes

Choose WAN Services to Meet Customer Requirements

On Day 24, "Evaluate Key Characteristics of WANs," you evaluated the key characteristics of WANs. Now you can view these characteristics with the intent to determine which type of WAN works best for a given situation. Modules 2 and 5 from CCNA 1, Module 1 from CCNA 2, and Modules 2, 3, 4, and 5 from CCNA 4 provide the content necessary to understand and choose a WAN service.

CCNA 1, Module 2

2.1.7 and 2.1.10—WANs connect LANs over a large geographically separated area using a modem on a plain old telephone service (POTS) line, Integrated Service Digital Network (ISDN), digital subscriber line (DSL), Frame Relay, Synchronous Optical Network (SONET), T1, E1, T3, or E3. WANs often provide access over serial interfaces at lower speeds than a LAN. A LAN can be extended through a public WAN using a virtual private network (VPN). A VPN provides a private network that exists inside of a public network. Clients connect through a secure tunnel to the VPN router at the destination.

CCNA 1, Module 5

5.2.1–5.2.6—WAN physical connections include serial, RJ-45, RJ-11, and F-connectors. Cisco High-Level Data Link Control (HDLC), Point-to-Point Protocol (PPP), and Frame Relay use serial connections and provide speeds ranging from 2400 bps to 1.54 Mbps for a T1 and 2.048 Mbps for an E1. You connect ISDN with an RJ-45 connector. ISDN basic rate interface (BRI) provides two 64 kbps bearer (B) channels and one 16 kbps delta (D) channel. Table 18-1 provides a brief description of how to cable WAN services.

Table 18-1   WAN Physical Connections

Connection Type	Physical Connectors	Cabling
Serial	60-pin or smart serial	The router connects to a channel service unit/data service unit (CSU/DSU) with a data terminal equipment (DTE) serial cable.
ISDN	BRI S/T BRI U	If a network termination 1 (NT1) device is needed, the router will connect with a BRI S/T interface. A BRI U interface includes the NT1.
DSL	RJ-11	Connect a DSL router using a standard RJ-11 phone connector and phone line.
Cable	F-connector	Connect a cable modem with a standard coaxial cable and F-connector.
Console	RJ-45 to DB-9	Use a rollover cable and connect to the RJ-45 console port on the router; then connect the DB-9 end to the serial port on a computer.

CCNA 2, Module 1

1.1.1–1.1.4—Connections and protocols specific to a WAN operate at OSI Layers 1 and 2. When you design a WAN, you will almost always coordinate with a communication service provider such as a local phone company and use routers, modems, and communication servers. Routers often act as a gateway from your LAN to a WAN. Make sure that the RAM, CPU, NVRAM, and router interfaces are capable of supporting the specific WAN service that you choose.

CCNA 4, Module 2

2.1.1 and 2.1.2—If you have selected a WAN service that uses a communication service provider, you are connected to the provider's nearest exchange, or central office (CO), over the local loop or last mile. In your building, the phone company provides you a port as the demarcation point. You commonly use a High-Speed Serial Interface (HSSI) to a CSU/DSU. A modem can also serve this purpose by modulating and then demodulating the signal in order to pass digital information over an analog line on the public switched telephone network (PSTN).

2.1.3—As review from Day 24, Table 18-2 displays the physical layer standards for a WAN, and Table 18-3 displays the data link layer standards for a WAN.

Table 18-2   WAN Physical Layer Standards

Standard	Speed
EIA/TIA-232	64 kbps
EIA/TIA-449/530	Up to 2 Mbps
EIA/TIA-612/613	HSSI up to 52 Mbps
V.35	48 kbps
X.21	Synchronous digital up to 64 kbps

Table 18-3   WAN Data Link Layer Protocols

Type	Protocol
Point-to-point	Cisco HDLC, PPP, Link Access Procedure Balanced (LAPB)
Packet switched	X.25, Frame Relay
Circuit switched	ISDN

2.1.4—The most common Layer 2 WAN encapsulation uses the HDLC standard. As discussed on Day 24, there are three types of HDLC frames:

- **Unnumbered frame**—This frame is for line setup messages.

- **Information frame**—This frame holds data.

- **Supervisory frame**—This frame controls data frame flow and can request retransmission if an error occurs.

2.1.5—The phone system requires continuous connections and is considered a circuit-switched system, but for data communication it is possible for many computers to share a connection and take turns requesting and receiving data as packets in short bursts. A connection that shares capacity by switching packets for many nodes is called a *packet-switched network (PSN)*. Packet-switched networks can be connectionless or connection-oriented, as outlined in the following two examples:

- The Internet is an example of a connectionless packet-switched system where each packet contains full addressing information.

- Frame Relay is an example of a Layer 2 WAN connection-oriented packet-switching system where the route is determined by switches and each frame carries an identifier called a data-link connection identifier (DLCI).

Frame Relay switches create a virtual circuit (VC) between communicating hosts that exists only when the frame is being transferred. You can refer to a temporary virtual circuit as a switched virtual circuit (SVC). When a virtual circuit needs to exist forever, it is called a permanent virtual circuit (PVC).

2.1.6—To connect to a WAN, you can use a dedicated circuit and buy a fractional T1/E1 through T3/E3 or DSL, or you can instead choose a switched circuit as one of the following:

- Circuit-switched in the form of ISDN or POTS

- Packet-switched in the form of X.25 or Frame Relay

- Cell-switched as Asynchronous Transfer Mode (ATM)

If you choose packet switching and if your bandwidth requirements are low, you can save money if you request an SVC instead of a PVC. With an SVC, the provider can allow you to share a physical link with other subscribers.

2.2.1–2.2.8—Table 18-4 provides a detailed menu of WAN services that you could serve to your client.

Table 18-4   WAN Service Menu

WAN Service	Media and Devices	Features
Analog dial-up	Modem uses copper and connects over the local loop to the PSTN.	Simple, highly available, low cost, low bandwidth, 56 kbps maximum bandwidth. Works well for e-mail and small reports. Intermittent connection over a dedicated circuit. Slower call setup than ISDN.
ISDN	ISDN modem uses the local loop as a digital connection to the provider.	BRI provides two 64 kbps B channels and one 16 kbps D channel. PRI provides 23 B channels and one 64 kbps D channel in the U.S., and 30 B channels and one D channel in other parts of the world. Quick setup using the D channel and high-bandwidth capabilities. Also serves as a backup for a leased line.

continues

Table 18-4   WAN Service Menu   *continued*

WAN Service	Media and Devices	Features
Leased line	Router serial port, CSU/DSU connection over copper or optical media.	Point-to-point permanent dedicated connection, fixed-capacity links with no latency or jitter. Cost is based on a fixed bandwidth; very expensive for a network with multiple endpoints.
X.25	Dial-up or leased-line connections to an X.25 network.	Packet-switched shared service that uses private or shared virtual circuits. Cost is based on the amount of bandwidth used and not a fixed bandwidth. Max 48 kbps bandwidth, often used for point-of-sale machines. Mostly replaced by Frame Relay, works at the network layer.
Frame Relay	Typically a leased line, but can also be dial-up to a Frame Relay network.	Works more efficiently than X.25 at the data link layer with frames and virtual circuits such as X.25. Up to 4 Mbps bandwidth maximum with the capability for a committed information rate (CIR) in a private virtual circuit. Frame Relay is a permanent shared connection.
ATM	Multiple virtual circuits can be provided over a single leased line.	Very fast permanent shared connection that operates using cells rather than frames. Standard 53-byte cell provides low latency at a maximum bandwidth above 155 Mbps. Offers both private and shared virtual circuits, with private virtual circuits being most common.
DSL	DSL modem copper phone lines over the local loop to a DSL Access Multiplexer (DLSAM).	Uses a higher frequency than the 4 kHz voice channel to send data allowing voice and data to transmit simultaneously. Allows for bandwidth up to 8.192 Mbps over many different varieties, including symmetric DSL (SDSL) and asymmetric DSL (ADSL). The local loop must be less than 5.5 kilometers (3.5 miles). DSL sends data across the Internet, so VPN is a common way to secure the connection.
Cable modem	Cable modem and coaxial cable connect to the Internet using existing television cabling.	Residential shared broadband access providing both television and network connectivity. Speeds up to 40 Mbps, often capped by the provider. Increase in neighborhood users can decrease bandwidth. A personal firewall and VPN provide security for transmission over the Internet.

2.3.1 and 2.3.2—Recall these key points and steps from Day 20, "Design a Simple Internetwork Using Cisco Technology," when you design the WAN portion of an internetwork:

- You will likely purchase your WAN connections from a communications provider for cost and legal reasons.

- You must balance the cost of WAN connections with the speed necessary for your WAN to function. WAN connections are slower than LAN connections but may need to support voice and video as well as data.

- WANs function at the lower three layers of the OSI model but focus on Layers 1 and 2.

As mentioned on Day 20, you should consider the following steps to design a WAN:

Step 1   Locate LANS.

Step 2   Analyze traffic.

Step 3   Plan a topology.

Step 4   Plan bandwidth.

Step 5   Choose technology.

Step 6   Evaluate cost.

2.3.3—The most common WAN design connects a main point to branch networks in a star topology. A partial mesh topology may also work well to provide better reliability. You would commonly use ISDN or DSL to connect a small office or home office (SOHO). You could choose Frame Relay or leased lines to connect larger branch offices to a WAN. A short leased line that connects each office to a Frame Relay network would cost much less than connecting each branch with long leased lines. If you need a high-bandwidth network with low latency, consider leased lines, ATM, or Frame Relay with a CIR or quality of service (QoS) mechanism. Remember that a shared service such as ATM or Frame Relay will cost less than a leased line.

2.3.4 and 2.3.5—If you had to connect 900 office branches, a flat WAN topology would not provide very good service. The three-layer hierarchical design provides an excellent structure for WAN design. If you are designing for a business, you can parallel the region, area, and branch with the core, distribution, and access layer design. The three-layer design helps you to better implement, scale, manage, and troubleshoot a WAN. An example design you could implement would be to connect branches with Frame Relay to regions that use an ATM backbone to connect to the main office. Use the structure of the three-layer model to help define bandwidth and organizational aspects of a WAN. You can always adjust the layers to fit your specific topology and focus on only two layers for a network that best fits that design.

2.3.6—How your WAN connects to the Internet is a key security factor in your design. If you connect to the Internet at an office only, then you have only one connection to secure, but all Internet traffic must pass over your WAN connections to branch offices. If each branch connects to the Internet, you have less WAN traffic but more vulnerable points on your WAN. Some companies tunnel WAN traffic only over Internet connections, which saves connectivity costs and enables more spending on added security.

CCNA 4, Module 3

3.1.1–3.1.4—WAN serial communication requires that frames are sent one bit at a time over the wire. Serial communication standards include RS-232-E, V.35, and HSSI. Multiple devices and users can connect with a single serial connection using time division multiplexing (TDM). Each transmitting device has a time slot on the serial connection that it can use to transmit. In the United States, you are responsible for maintaining the CSU/DSU at the demarcation point. A router that you connect to the CSU/DSU is considered the customer premises equipment (CPE). In other countries, the network terminating unit (NTU) is managed by the communications provider.

Typically, your CPE router is considered the DTE, and the communication provider has the DCE equipment and provides clocking.

3.1.5—Cisco HDLC encapsulation, as mentioned previously in the section "CCNA 4, Module 2" under 2.1.4, is the default Layer 2 encapsulation for a serial link and defines an unnumbered, information, and supervisory frame. Cisco HDLC uses synchronous serial transmission and supports multiple protocols using a proprietary type field as a Layer 3 protocol field.

3.2.1–3.2.6—PPP is a layered protocol that provides transmission for multiple network layer protocols and tests connectivity using the data link layer. You can configure PPP to operate on asynchronous serial, synchronous serial, HSSI, and ISDN. PPP uses the Link Control Protocol (LCP) to establish the link and the Network Control Protocol (NCP) to configure the Layer 3 protocols. LCP includes the following options:

- **Authentication**—You can require the device making the call to authenticate using the clear text Password Authentication Protocol (PAP) or the more secure and encrypted Challenge Handshake Authentication Protocol (CHAP). PAP authenticates only once, while CHAP frequently rechecks the authentication.

- **Compression**—This option can increase throughput on the link, and the receiving device decompresses the frames. Stacker and Predictor are two types of compression available on a Cisco router.

- **Error detection**—Quality and Magic Number options can help keep the link reliable.

- **Multilink**—This option allows for load balancing over multiple PPP-configured router interfaces. This feature is available with Cisco IOS Software Release 11.1 and later.

- **PPP callback**—This security feature allows the client to first call and then request the router to call back with a specific configuration. This feature is available with Cisco IOS Software Release 11.1 and later.

NCP uses a separate protocol to control each network layer protocol. An example would be that, for IP, NCP uses IP Control Protocol (IPCP). A PPP frame consists of a flag field, an address field, a control field, a protocol field, a data field, and a frame check sequence (FCS) field. Table 18-5 describes each of the phases of the PPP session establishment.

Table 18-5   PPP Session Establishment

Phase	Description
Link establishment phase	Each device sends LCP frames, and they negotiate LCP options; then LCP opens the connection with a configuration acknowledgment frame.
Authentication phase (optional)	The established link can authenticate using PAP or CHAP and also check link quality.
Network layer protocol phase	PPP devices send NCP packets to configure network layer protocols and allow Layer 3 transmission.

Inactivity timers, user intervention, and NCP or LCP frames can close a PPP link.

CCNA 4, Module 4

4.1.1–4.1.3—Local carriers use ISDN to provide a digital connection on the local loop for a subscriber that allows you to exceed the 56 kbps bandwidth barrier of an analog connection. ISDN BRI has two B channels at 64 kbps for data and one D channel at 16 kbps for call setup. ISDN can use PPP encapsulation. The three categories for ISDN protocols are as follows:

- **E Series**—Telephone network standards

- **I Series**—ISDN concepts and terminology

- **Q Series**—How switching and call setup (signaling) function, including Q.921 link access procedure on the D channel (LAPD) and the Q.931 ISDN network layer

ISDN uses out-of-band signaling, which means that the D channel handles call setup using LAPD outside of the data paths in the B channels. As described in Table 18-4, ISDN can provide 2 B channels and 1 D channel with BRI or 23 B channels and 1 D channel with PRI. Outside of America and Japan, PRI offers 30 B channels. ISDN PRI provides the same service as a T1/E1 connection. Table 18-6 outlines the fields of an ISDN frame.

Table 18-6   ISDN Frame Fields

Field	Description
Flag	Beginning of the frame.
Address	Contains the following information:
	Service access point identifier (SAPI)—Identifies the Layer 3 portal
	Command and response (C/R) bit—Identifies whether the frame has a command or response bit
	Extended addressing (EA) bits—Identifies if the address is 1 byte or 2 bytes
	Terminal endpoint identifier (TEI)—Unique equipment identifier
Control	Similar to HDLC.
Data	Encapsulated data for upper layers.
FCS	Frame Check Sequence allows a check for damaged frames using a cyclic redundancy check (CRC).
Flag	End of the frame.

4.1.4—To establish a BRI or PRI call, the D channel first sends the called number to the ISDN switch. The local switch uses the Signaling System 7 (SS7) signaling to set up a path. The remote switch signals the destination over the D channel. The destination NT1 device sends the remote ISDN switch a call-connect message, and the remote ISDN switch uses SS7 to send a call-connect to the local switch. The local switch connects one B channel for end-to-end communication. The other B channel is available for a later connection. In essence, ISDN switches use the D channel and SS7 signaling to establish data links on the B channel.

4.1.5—The ISDN reference points on a chart resemble alphabet soup. Either you have a terminal equipment 1 (TE1) device with a native ISDN interface or a terminal equipment 2 (TE2) device that requires a terminal adapter (TA) to connect to ISDN. The following two written examples and Figure 18-1 depict each of the ISDN reference point locations based on your TE1 or TE2:

- You have a TE1 that is a native ISDN interface that connects at the S reference to the customer switching network termination type 2 (NT2). The NT2 connects at the T reference to the network termination type 1 (NT1), and the NT1 connects at the U reference to the local loop.

- You have a TE2 that is nonnative ISDN, so you first connect at the R reference to the TA and then to the NT2. The NT2 connects at the T reference to the NT1, and the NT1 connects at the U reference to the local loop.

S and T references can be similar, so you may sometimes see an S/T interface.

Figure 18-1   ISDN Reference Points

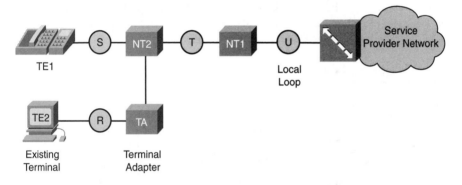

4.1.6 and 4.1.7—When determining the appropriate ISDN interface on a router, remember the following:

- Look at the back of the router and determine if there is a BRI interface or BRI WAN interface card (WIC).

- Determine whether or not you have to provide the NT1 device to terminate the local loop to the CO. In the United States, you will have to provide the NT1; in other countries, the provider supplies the NT1.

- If the router has a U interface, the NT1 is built in, but if the router has an S/T interface, it needs an external connector.

- If the router has a BRI interface and does not have an NT1 built in, it will need to connect to an NT1.

- If the router has only serial interfaces, it is a TE2 and will need a TA to connect to the NT1.

To connect to the provider, make sure that you have the switch type and the service profile identifiers (SPIDs) for the provider. SPIDs are used in North America and Japan to identify the B channel. SPIDs resemble phone numbers.

CCNA 4, Module 5

5.1.1—Frame Relay is a packet-switched, connection-oriented, data link layer WAN technology. Frame Relay uses a subset of HDLC called Link Access Procedure for Frame Relay (LAPF) for encapsulation. Once the frame is forwarded from the DTE router to a DCE Frame Relay switch, the network of Frame Relay switches moves the data to its destination. Typically, you will subscribe to a network of trunked Frame Relay switches owned by a public carrier.

5.1.2—The following process would allow you to connect LAN1 to LAN2 across town using Frame Relay:

1. You call the phone company and connect your LAN1 router to their nearest Frame Relay switch. Your LAN1 router will have a unique DLCI that identifies it on the Frame Relay switch network.

2. You then connect the LAN2 router to a nearby Frame Relay switch on the same phone company network. LAN2 will also have a DLCI that identifies it on the Frame Relay network.

3. The phone company uses its Frame Relay switches to then establish a packet-switched PVC across town for your two LANs.

4. The routers on LAN1 and LAN2 operate as Frame Relay access devices (FRADs).

5.1.3—Frame Relay receives a packet from a Layer 3 protocol and encapsulates it as a Layer 2 frame to transfer over the Frame Relay network. If a frame does not match its FCS upon delivery, the frame is simply dropped and error control is left for the upper layers.

5.1.4—Your initial connection to a Frame Relay network will commonly be over a leased line. The provider determines the bandwidth of the leased line and can also provide a CIR for your PVC on the Frame Relay network. It is possible for your network to use more than your CIR on the Frame Relay network, but every allowed frame that is over the CIR will be marked as discard eligible (DE) with a 1 in the DE bit of the address field. These DE frames will be dropped first if congestion occurs. Frame Relay switches avoid congestion by using an explicit congestion notification (ECN) bit in the frame address field. The Frame Relay switch will set the Forward ECN (FECN) bit and Backward ECN (BECN) bit on received and sent frames to notify the DTEs to reduce flow.

5.1.5—Routers that you connect to a Frame Relay network receive a DLCI to identify the virtual circuit (VC). You can configure a physical interface to support multiple VCs and multiple DLCIs. Remember that the DLCI for each VC must be associated with the network address of its remote router. The DLCI associations or mappings can be configured using map commands or automatically with inverse ARP.

5.1.6—The 10-bit DLCI field in a Frame Relay frame permits VC identifiers 0 through 1023. Some of these identifiers are reserved for link management identifiers (LMIs). LMIs allow DTEs to exchange information and dynamically learn information about the status of the network. Cisco routers support Cisco, ANSI, and Q933a-type LMIs. LMI 0 is used by ANSI and q933a, and LMI 1023 is used by Cisco. LMI messages are slightly different from the regular LAPF frames. LMI frames include information about the status of a DLCI.

5.1.7—A router that is connected to a Frame Relay network will send LMI status inquiry messages to the network. The network responds with details of every VC configured on the link. The router can map VCs to network layer addresses by sending an inverse ARP message to each VC and including its own network layer address. The connected router can use the inverse ARP replies to populate its DLCI map table. A router will send inverse ARP messages for each network layer protocol.

Summary

Whether you decide to use dial-up, ISDN, Frame Relay, or two cans and a string, you will at some point be required to defend your decision. Your well-rounded knowledge of the physical, logical, and design aspects of each WAN service will serve you well. You will probably have to talk about cost, but that changes regularly and is not covered in the CCNA. You can review everything but WAN costs in a more flashy format by reading pages 174–196, 488–502, 520–532, and 548–564 in the *CCNA Flash Cards and Exam Practice Pack* (CCNA Self-Study, exam #640-801), Second Edition.

Your Notes

Part III

17–9 Days Before the Exam—Implementation and Operation

Day 17: Configure Routing Protocols Given User Requirements

Day 16: Configure IP Addresses, Subnet Masks, and Gateway Addresses on Routers and Hosts

Day 15: Configure a Router for Additional Administrative Functionality

Day 14: Configure a Switch with VLANs and Interswitch Communication

Day 13: Implement a LAN

Day 12: Customize a Switch Configuration to Meet Specified Requirements and Manage System Image and Device Configuration Files (Two Objectives)

Day 11: Perform an Initial Configuration on a Router and Perform an Initial Configuration on a Switch (Two Objectives)

Day 10: Implement Access Lists

Day 9: Implement Simple WAN Protocols

Configure Routing Protocols Given User Requirements

The configuration and troubleshooting CCNA exam objectives that introduce configuration commands in this book will provide a quick definition for a set of commands, as well as the syntax and examples. These chapters help you to recognize and remember the commands. On the CCNA exam, you will encounter portions of a routing configuration and partial sets of commands. It is very important that you become accustomed to recognizing the command mode from the prompt. The days that cover configuration and troubleshooting will help you to quickly orient your knowledge while reading snippets of configuration information. To master these commands, you should also practice with a simulator, the e-labs, or even better, on real routers at your academy. Do not practice on your gateway router at work.

Routing protocol configurations will only work once you have configured the interfaces on a router. You will cover interface configuration on a Day 16, "Configure IP Addresses, Subnet Masks, and Gateway Addresses on Routers and Hosts." Most routing configurations start in global configuration mode. Modules 1, 6, and 7 from CCNA 2 and Modules 1, 2, and 3 from CCNA 3 discuss routing protocol configurations.

Today, you review the syntax for a routing protocol configuration and see examples of how the commands should look in the command-line interface (CLI). Consider the information provided here a primer for hands-on review in the lab or with a simulator.

CCNA 2, Module 1

1.1.3—When you have connected all the cables and devices that constitute a WAN, you should keep the following points in mind as you configure the routers:

- Maintain consistent addressing that represents your network topologies.

- Use protocols that will select the best path.

- Use dynamic routing for ease of configuration and static routes for specific routing needs.

CCNA 2, Module 6

6.1.3—The syntax for a static route follows:

    ip route destination-network subnet-mask {outgoing-interface | next-hop-address}

Example 17-1   Configuring a Static Route

```
Router(config)#ip route 192.168.1.0 255.255.255.0 192.168.1.2
```

6.1.4—The syntax for a default route follows:

```
ip route 0.0.0.0 0.0.0.0 {outgoing-interface ¦ next-hop-address}
```

Example 17-2   Configuring a Default Route

```
Router(config)#ip route 0.0.0.0 0.0.0.0 s0
```

6.1.5—The commands shown in Example 17-3 allow you to check your static and default routes.

Example 17-3   Verifying Static and Default Routes

```
Router#show running-config
Router#show ip route
```

CCNA 2, Module 7

7.2.2—The syntax to enable and configure Routing Information Protocol (RIP) is as follows:

```
router rip
network directly-connected-network
```

Example 17-4   Configuring RIP

```
Router(config)#router rip
Router(config-router)#network 192.168.1.0
Router(config-router)#network 192.168.2.0
```

7.2.3—The **ip classless** command shown in Example 17-5 allows a router to ignore network class boundaries. The **ip classless** command is on by default on most routers.

Example 17-5   The ip classless Command

```
Router(config)#ip classless
```

7.2.7—The following command syntax prevents routing updates from transmitting on an interface:

```
router rip
passive-interface interface
```

Example 17-6   The passive-interface Command

```
Router(config)#router rip
Router(config-router)#passive-interface fa0/0
```

7.2.8 and 7.2.9—RIP can load balance traffic over up to six network paths. The following command sets the number of paths:

```
router rip
maximum-paths {0-6}
```

Example 17-7   Setting Load Balancing Maximum Paths

```
Router(config)#router rip
Router(config-router)#maximum-paths 3
```

To tell a router to load balance on a per-packet basis rather than a per-destination basis, use the following syntax:

```
interface interface
no ip route-cache
```

Example 17-8   Setting an Interface to Route on a Per-Packet Basis

```
Router(config)#interface s0/0
Router(config-if)#no ip route-cache
```

7.2.10—You can dictate the priority of a route using the administrative distance (AD). The following command increases the AD of a static route to 130 so that a dynamic route with an AD of 120 will take priority in the routing table. You add the administrative distance option to the end of your static route configuration.

Example 17-9   Configuring a Static Route with an Administrative Distance

```
Router(config)#ip route 192.168.1.0 255.255.255.0 192.168.1.2 130
```

You can also remove a static route by adding a **no** in front of the command, as shown in Example 17-10.

Example 17-10 Removing a Static Route

```
Router(config)#no ip route 192.168.1.0 255.255.255.0 192.168.1.2
```

7.3.5—The following commands allow you to enable and configure Interior Gateway Routing Protocol (IGRP):

```
router igrp autonomous-system-number
network directly-connected-network
```

Example 17-11 Configuring IGRP

```
Router(config)#router igrp 101
Router(config-router)#network 192.168.1.0
Router(config-router)#network 192.168.2.0
```

7.3.6 and 7.3.7—IGRP has an administrative distance of 100 and will take priority over RIP entries in a routing table. If you have a router with both protocols configured, you can view information about the protocols and verify IGRP configuration with the commands shown in Example 17-12.

Example 17-12 Viewing Configured Protocols

```
Router#show ip protocols
Router#show ip route
Router#show running-config
Router#show interface
```

CCNA 3, Module 1

1.1.6—Although variable-length subnet mask (VLSM) support is a component of a routing protocol, you need to configure the interface with the proper subnet mask in order for routing with VLSM to work properly. The configuration of the correct mask allows the routing protocol to advertise the right mask with each network. You would use the following interface configuration syntax on a serial interface with a point-to-point connection that requires only a two-host network:

```
ip address ip-address subnet-mask
```

Example 17-13 Configuring an Interface with VLSM

```
Router(config)#interface serial 0
Router(config-if)#ip address 192.168.0.2 255.255.255.252
```

Once you have configured all the interfaces with the proper subnet masks, you can configure a routing protocol such as RIP version 2 that supports VLSM.

1.2.4 and 1.2.5—RIP version 2 configuration syntax is as follows:

```
router rip
version 2
network directly-connected-network
```

Example 17-14 Configuring RIP Version 2

```
Router(config)#router rip
Router(config-router)#version 2
Router(config-router)#network 192.168.1.0
```

Just as with RIP and IGRP, you can verify RIP version 2 configuration with the commands listed previously in Example 17-12.

CCNA 3, Module 2

2.3.1—The following is the command syntax for Open Shortest Path First (OSPF):

```
router ospf process-id
network network-address wildcard-mask area area-id
```

Example 17-15 Configuring OSPF

```
Router(config)#router ospf 1
Router(config-router)#network 192.168.1.0 0.0.0.255 area 0
Router(config-router)#network 192.168.2.0 0.0.0.255 area 0
```

2.3.2—OSPF uses the highest local IP address as its router ID unless a loopback interface exists, in which case the highest loopback IP address will become the router ID. Loopbacks are used to ensure that a router always has an active interface. The loopback interface should be configured with a host mask, which is a 32-bit mask. The following command configures the loopback interface to guarantee OSPF reliability:

```
ip address ip-address subnet-mask
```

Example 17-16 Configuring the Loopback Interface with a Host Mask

```
Router(config)#interface loopback 0
Router(config-if)#ip address 192.168.0.9 255.255.255.255
```

All OSPF routers have a default priority of zero, and the highest priority wins. To control the designated router election process, you can set the OSPF priority with the following configuration:

```
ip ospf priority {0-255}
```

Example 17-17 Configuring the OSPF Router Priority

```
Router(config)#interface serial 0
Router(config-if)#ip ospf priority 40
```

You can verify OSPF priority configuration with the following command:

```
show ip ospf priority interface interface
```

Example 17-18 Verifying the OSPF Router Priority Configuration

```
Router(config)#show ip ospf interface serial 0
```

2.3.3—You can control the priority of an OSPF route by adjusting the bandwidth and cost. OSPF automatically calculates the interface cost based on bandwidth. Altering the bandwidth alters the cost. You can override this calculation by manually setting the cost. You can control the priority of the link on your network with the following commands:

```
bandwidth bandwidth
ip ospf cost {1-65,535}
```

Example 17-19 Configuring the Bandwidth of an Interface

```
Router(config)#interface serial 0
Router(config-if)#bandwidth 64
```

Example 17-20 Configuring the OSPF Cost for an Interface

```
Router(config)#interface serial 0
Router(config-if)#ip ospf cost 1
```

2.3.4—The following commands will configure simple OSPF authentication:

```
ip ospf authentication-key password
area area-number authentication
```

Example 17-21 Configuring Simple OSPF Authentication

```
Router(config)#interface serial 0
Router(config-if)#ip ospf authentication-key cisco
Router(config-if)#exit
Router(config)#router ospf 1
Router(dhcp-config)#area 0 authentication
```

The following commands configure OSPF authentication with MD5 encryption:

```
ip ospf message-digest-key key-id md5 key
area area-number authentication message-digest
```

Example 17-22 Configuring OSPF Authentication with MD5 Encryption

```
Router(config)#interface serial 0
Router(config-if)#ip ospf message-digest-key 1 md5 cisco
Router(config-if)#exit
Router(config)#router ospf 1
Router(dhcp-config)#area 0 authentication message-digest
```

2.3.5—You must have the same hello and dead timer intervals in OSPF in order for your routers to exchange information. The default values are 10 seconds for a hello and 40 seconds for a dead interval timer. These values work fine, but if you would like, you can change them with the following commands:

```
ip ospf hello-interval seconds
ip ospf dead-interval seconds
```

Example 17-23 Configuring OSPF Hello and Dead Intervals

```
Router(config)#interface serial 0
Router(config-if)#ip ospf hello-interval 5
Router(config-if)#ip ospf hello-interval 20
```

2.3.6—To add a default route and then propagate that route with OSPF, use the following commands:

```
ip route 0.0.0.0 0.0.0.0 {interface ¦next-hop-address}
default-information originate
```

Example 17-24 Propagating a Default Route with OSPF

```
Router(config)#ip route 0.0.0.0 0.0.0.0 serial 0
Router(config)#router ospf 1
Router(config-router)#default-information originate
```

2.3.7–2.3.8—You can check OSPF operation and configuration using the following **show**, **clear**, and **debug** commands:

```
show ip protocol
show ip route
show ip ospf interface
show ip ospf
show ip ospf neighbor detail
show ip ospf database
clear ip route *
clear ip route next-hop-address
debug ip ospf events
debug ip ospf adj
```

CCNA 3, Module 3

3.2.1—The following commands enable Enhanced Interior Gateway Routing Protocol (EIGRP) and configure bandwidth and logging:

```
router eigrp autonomous-system-number
network network-number
eigrp log-neighbor-changes
```

Example 17-25 Configuring EIGRP and Logging

```
Router(config)#router eigrp 10
Router(config-router)#network 192.168.1.0
Router(config-router)#network 192.168.2.0
Router(config-router)#eigrp log-neighbor-changes
```

The following command configures EIGRP bandwidth:

```
bandwidth bandwidth
```

Example 17-26 Configuring EIGRP Bandwidth

```
Router(config)#interface serial 0
Router(config-if)#bandwidth 56
```

3.2.2—If you want to turn off route summary in EIGRP for subnets that are not continuous, you can use the following command:

```
no auto-summary
```

Example 17-27 Turning Off EIGRP Route Summarization

```
Router(config)#router eigrp 10
Router(config-router)#no auto-summary
```

You can also manually configure a summary address with the following command:

```
ip summary-address eigrp as-number ip-address mask administrative-distance
```

Example 17-28 Manually Configuring EIGRP Route Summarization

```
Router(config)#interface serial 0
Router(config-if)#ip summary-address eigrp 10 172.16.0.0 255.255.0.0
```

3.2.3—The following **show** commands allow you to verify EIGRP:

```
show ip eigrp neighbors
show ip eigrp interfaces
show ip eigrp topology
```

3.2.4–3.2.7—As discussed on Day 28, "Evaluate the Characteristics of Routing Protocols," EIGRP uses the diffusing update algorithm (DUAL) to maintain a neighbor table and topology table of available routes. The *successor route* is considered the best route and is added to the topology table as well as the routing table. A backup route called the *feasible successor* is kept in the topology table.

Summary

The configurations for RIP, IGRP, OSPF, and EIGRP should at this point be easy to recognize and use if you intend to be CCNA test ready. Skimming through these examples will help jog your memory, but sitting at a router or simulator will internalize the steps and commands. Pages 388–454 from the *CCNA Flash Cards and Exam Practice Pack* (CCNA Self-Study, exam #640-801), Second Edition, can give you a great overview of everything "routy," from concepts to configuration.

Your Notes

Configure IP Addresses, Subnet Masks, and Gateway Addresses on Routers and Hosts

A minute to configure, a lifetime to address. Your knowledge of IP addressing, subnetting, routing protocols, and variable-length subnet masks (VLSMs) converge when you decide to configure an IP address and mask on your router interface. The configuration is simple and short, but the masks and interface addresses you choose for your routers are pillars in your logical network design. Modules 1 and 9 from CCNA 1, Module 3 from CCNA 2, and Modules 1 and 2 from CCNA 3 outline the various interface configuration commands. Today, you review the syntax for interface-related configuration commands and see examples of how the commands should look in the command-line interface (CLI). Consider the information provided here a primer for hands-on review in the lab or with a simulator.

CCNA 1, Module 1

1.1.6—Routers and hosts use TCP/IP to communicate across a network. You need to configure IP addresses and subnet masks on both hosts and routers to complete a network. You can assign an address to a host using the operating system or configure the host to obtain the IP address automatically. To configure an IP on a router interface, you can use Cisco IOS software.

CCNA 1, Module 9

9.2.1–9.2.7—On Day 27, "Evaluate the TCP/IP Communication Process and Its Associated Protocols," and Day 22, "Design an IP Addressing Scheme to Meet Design Requirements," you reviewed the proper dotted decimal format for an IP address and subnet masks. Remember to apply the conventions in IP addressing covered on those days when you configure the interfaces on a router and your network hosts.

CCNA 2, Module 3

3.1.1—To use the CLI on a router, you must know the hierarchy of configuration modes. Figure 16-1 and Table 16-1 provide examples of the modes available to you for router configuration.

Figure 16-1   Router Modes

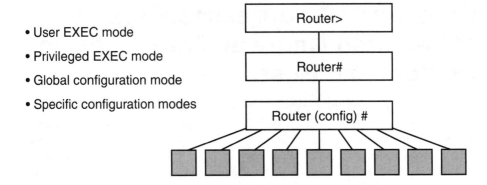

- User EXEC mode
- Privileged EXEC mode
- Global configuration mode
- Specific configuration modes

Table 16-1   Configuration Modes and Prompts

Configuration Mode	Prompt
Interface	Router(config-if)#
Subinterface	Router(config-subif)#
Controller	Router(config-controller)#
Map-list	Router(config-map-list)#
Map-class	Router(config-map-class)#
Line	Router(config-line)#
Router	Router(config-router)#
IPX-router	Router(config-ipx-router)#
Route-map	Router(config-route-map)#

Example 16-1 shows the commands you would use to enter interface configuration mode.

Example 16-1   Entering Interface Configuration Mode for Serial 0

```
Router>enable
Router#configure terminal
Router(config)#interface serial 0
Router(config-if)#
```

3.1.5—You use the following command syntax to configure a serial interface. You use the **clock rate** command only if you are configuring a data communications equipment (DCE) interface.

```
interface type slot/port
ip address ip-address netmask
clock rate clock-rate
no shutdown
```

Example 16-2   Configuring a Serial Interface

```
Router(config)#interface serial 0/0
Router(config-if)#ip address 172.16.1.1 255.255.255.0
Router(config-if)#clock rate 56000
Router(config-if)#no shutdown
```

3.1.6—You can use the **no** form of a command to remove the configuration. Example 16-3 would remove the IP address and clock rate from the interface configured in Example 16-2 and shut down the interface.

Example 16-3   Removing Previously Entered Configurations

```
Router(config)#interface serial 0/0
Router(config-if)#no ip address 172.16.1.1 255.255.255.0
Router(config-if)#no clock rate 56000
Router(config-if)#shutdown
```

You can always check your entire configuration, including all interface configurations, and save the configuration to nonvolatile RAM (NVRAM) by using the following commands in global configuration mode:

```
show running-config
copy running-config startup-config
```

3.1.7—You use the following command set to configure an Ethernet interface:

```
interface type slot/port
ip address ip-address netmask
no shutdown
```

Example 16-4   Configuring an Ethernet Interface

```
Router(config)#interface fastethernet 0/0
Router(config-if)#ip address 172.16.2.1 255.255.255.0
Router(config-if)#no shutdown
```

3.2.1–3.2.3—Keeping good standardized documentation of your router configurations is imperative for an organized network. A good start is to add a description to each interface so that you or anyone configuring the router can quickly identify the purpose and location of the interface. The following commands allow you to add an interface description:

```
interface type slot/port
description interface-description
```

Example 16-5   Configuring a Description for an Ethernet Interface

```
Router(config)#interface fastethernet 0
Router(config-if)#description Accounting LAN, Floor 11
```

When you have completed an interface configuration, you can change modes back to privileged exec quickly using Ctrl-Z, or by entering the **end** command. Also remember to copy your running configuration to NVRAM in order to save the changes you have made.

CCNA 3, Module 1

1.1.6—As discussed on Day 17, "Configure Routing Protocols Given User Requirements," you can configure routers with VLSM in networks to more efficiently use IP addresses. Make sure that your router is running a routing protocol that supports VLSM. You might use the configurations in Examples 16-6 and 16-7 if you were running RIP version 2 and only needed two IP addresses for a serial point-to-point link and a 12-host network for a LAN.

Example 16-6   Configuring a Serial Interface for a Point-to-Point Link

```
Router(config)#interface serial 0
Router(config-if)#ip address 172.16.0.2 255.255.255.252
```

Example 16-7   Configuring an Ethernet Interface for a 12-Host LAN

```
Router(config)#interface ethernet 0
Router(config-if)#ip address 172.16.0.17 255.255.255.240
```

CCNA 3, Module 2

2.3.2—As mentioned on Day 17, Open Shortest Path First (OSPF) cannot function reliably without an interface that is always active. You configure the loopback interface on an OSPF router to ensure that you have an always-active interface. If you have more than one loopback device configured, OSPF will use the highest loopback IP address as the router ID.

Example 16-8   Configuring the Loopback Interface with a Host Mask

```
Router(config)#interface loopback 0
Router(config-if)#ip address 192.168.0.9 255.255.255.255
```

Summary

Routing protocols function properly only if interfaces are configured properly. While you are practicing commands and taking curriculum practice exams, be sure to pay attention to the command mode for each command that you encounter. You will find questions concerning command modes and interface configuration mixed in with a few other commands on pages 198–238 in the *CCNA Flash Cards and Exam Practice Pack* (CCNA Self-Study, exam #640-801), Second Edition.

Your Notes

Configure a Router for Additional Administrative Functionality

Although Layer 3 path selection is the key function of a router, there are many other parameters that you can configure. The CCNA exam covers password configuration as well as Dynamic Host Configuration Protocol (DHCP), network address translation (NAT), and port address translation (PAT) configurations. Module 3 from CCNA 2 and Modules 1 and 6 from CCNA 4 provide additional configurations for your router.

Today, you review the syntax for password, DHCP, NAT, and PAT configuration commands and see examples of how the commands should look in the command-line interface (CLI). Consider today's information a primer for hands-on review in the lab or with a simulator.

CCNA 2, Module 3

3.1.2—The following command allows you to set a router hostname:

```
hostname hostname
```

Example 15-1   Configuring a Router Hostname

```
Router(config)#hostname Portland
Portland(config)#
```

3.1.3—You can restrict console access to a router with the following command:

```
password password
login
```

Example 15-2   Setting the Console Password

```
Router(config)#line console 0
Router(config-line)#password cisco
Router(config-line)#login
```

If you intend to access a router using Telnet, you will need to set the virtual terminal password, as follows:

```
password password
login
```

Example 15-3   Setting the VTY Password

```
Router(config)#line vty 0 4
Router(config-line)#password cisco
Router(config-line)#login
```

To restrict access to privileged EXEC mode, you must use the following command:

    enable password *password*

Example 15-4   Setting the Password for Privileged EXEC

```
Router(config)#enable password class
```

To encrypt and set the privileged EXEC password, use the following command:

    enable secret *password*

Example 15-5   Setting the Console Password

```
Router(config)#enable secret class
```

To encrypt all unencrypted passwords, use the following command:

    service *password-encryption*

Example 15-6   Encrypting all Unencrypted Passwords

```
Router(config)#service password-encryption
```

3.1.4—The following **show** commands provide you with information about the files, access, settings, and configuration of a router:

- **show interfaces**—Displays interface information

- **show controllers serial**—Displays interface hardware information

- **show clock**—Displays router time settings

- **show hosts**—Displays hostname and address cache

- **show users**—Displays connected users

- **show history**—Displays previously entered commands

- **show flash**—Displays flash memory and Cisco IOS file information

- **show version**—Displays information about the loaded operating system as well as hardware information

- **show arp**—Displays the Address Resolution Protocol (ARP) table

- **show protocols**—Displays information about presently configured Layer 3 protocols

- **show startup-config**—Displays the configuration saved in the NVRAM

- **show running-config**—Displays the running configuration in RAM

3.2.4 and 3.2.5—You use the following commands to display a message before a user logs in to the router:

```
banner motd delimiting-character
banner-message
delimiting-character
```

Example 15-7   Setting a Login Banner

```
Router(config)#banner motd #
Authorized Access Only
#
```

3.2.6 and 3.2.7—To associate a name with one or multiple IP addresses on a router, you can use the following command:

```
ip host {name} {IP-address}
```

Example 15-8   Associating a Name with an IP Address

```
Router(config)#ip host boise 192.168.1.33 192.168.2.1
```

You can test your configuration by using the **ping** command with the new hostnames on the router that you have configured, as shown in Example 15-9.

Example 15-9   Associating a Name with an IP Address

```
Router#ping boise
```

CCNA 4, Module 1

1.1.4—Static NAT is designed to allow one-to-one mapping of local and global addresses. To configure static NAT, you have to add a static NAT entry and then label the outside and inside interfaces using the following commands:

```
ip nat inside source static local-IP-address global-IP-address
ip nat outside
ip nat inside
```

Example 15-10 Configuring Static NAT

```
Router(config)#ip nat inside source static 192.168.1.5 209.165.200.226
Router(config)#interface serial 0
Router(config-if)#ip nat outside
Router(config-if)#interface fa 0/0
Router(config-if)#ip nat inside
```

To configure dynamic NAT, you define a pool of global addresses and then use an access list to define the range of inside addresses that are eligible to be converted with the following commands:

```
ip nat pool pool-name start-IP-address end-IP-address netmask netmask
access-list access-list-number permit inside-network wildcard-mask
```

Example 15-11 Defining Inside and Outside Addresses for Dynamic NAT Configuration

```
Router(config)#ip nat pool isp-pool 209.165.200.225 209.165.200.235 netmask
255.255.255.224
Router(config)#access-list 1 permit 192.168.1.0 0.0.0.255
```

Once you have defined a pool of outside addresses and a range of inside addresses with an access list, you set NAT to use the two groups for translation with the following commands:

```
ip nat inside source list access-list-number pool pool-name
ip nat outside
ip nat inside
```

Example 15-12 Configuring Dynamic NAT

```
Router(config)#ip nat inside source list 1 pool isp-pool
Router(config)#interface serial 0
Router(config-if)#ip nat outside
Router(config-if)#interface fa 0/0
Router(config-if)#ip nat inside
```

If you configure NAT with overload, you have enabled PAT. You can configure overload to translate many addresses to just one outside IP address that is assigned to an interface using the following commands:

```
access-list access-list-number permit inside-network wildcard-mask
ip nat inside source list access-list-number interface interface overload
ip nat outside
ip nat inside
```

Example 15-13 Configuring NAT with Overload for One Outside IP Address

```
Router(config)#access-list 1 permit 192.168.1.0 0.0.0.255
Router(config)#ip nat inside source list 1 interface serial 0 overload
Router(config)#interface serial 0
Router(config-if)#ip nat outside
Router(config-if)#interface fa 0/0
Router(config-if)#ip nat inside
```

You can also configure NAT with overload to translate a pool of addresses using the following commands:

```
access-list access-list-number permit inside-network wildcard-mask
ip nat pool pool-name start-IP-address end-IP-address netmask netmask
ip nat inside source list access-list-number pool pool-name overload
ip nat outside
ip nat inside
```

Example 15-14 Configuring NAT with Overload for a Pool of Outside IP Addresses

```
Router(config)#access-list 1 permit 192.168.1.0 0.0.0.255
Router(config)#ip nat pool isp-pool 209.165.200.225 209.165.200.235 netmask
255.255.255.224
Router(config)#ip nat inside source list 1 pool isp-pool overload
Router(config)#interface serial 0
Router(config-if)#ip nat outside
Router(config-if)#interface fa 0/0
Router(config-if)#ip nat inside
```

1.1.5—You can verify NAT and PAT configurations with the following commands:

```
show ip nat translations
show ip nat statistics
show running-config
```

1.1.6—You can also watch every packet that is translated in NAT with the following commands:

```
debug ip nat
debug ip nat detailed
```

1.2.4—You can configure a router to handle host addressing on your LAN with DHCP. As a DHCP server, the router can provide host machines with configurations such as an IP address, a DNS server, and lease time.

1.2.5—To configure DHCP on a router, you first define the DHCP pool and then provide other TCP/IP parameters with the following commands:

```
ip dhcp pool pool-name
network network-address subnet-mask
default-router default-router-address
dns-server dns-server-address
netbios-name-server netbios-name-server-address
domain-name domain-name
```

Example 15-15 Configuring DHCP

```
Router(config)#ip dhcp pool subnet4
Router(dhcp-config)#network 192.168.4.0 255.255.255.0
Router(dhcp-config)#default-router 192.168.4.254
Router(dhcp-config)#dns-server 192.168.4.2
Router(dhcp-config)#netbios-name-server 192.168.4.3
Router(dhcp-config)#domain-name bennettsupport.com
```

You can exclude a range of addresses or a single address from the DHCP pool that you wish to reserve and assign to specific hosts with the following commands:

```
ip dhcp excluded-address start-address end-address
ip dhcp excluded-address single-address
```

Example 15-16 DHCP Pool Excluded Address Range or Specific Addresses

```
Router(config)#ip dhcp pool excluded-address 192.168.4.1 192.168.4.20
Router(config)#ip dhcp pool excluded-address 192.168.4.254
```

You can start and stop the DHCP service with these two commands:

```
service dhcp
no service dhcp
```

1.2.6 and 1.2.7—To make sure that DHCP is operating, use the **show ip dhcp binding** command, which is shown in Example 15-17. Make sure that you test all **show** commands in a lab or simulation so that you are familiar with the output.

Example 15-17 Displaying DHCP Bindings

```
Router#show ip dhcp binding
```

You can also verify that the router is sending and receiving DHCP messages with the **show ip dhcp server statistics** command, which is shown in Example 15-18.

Example 15-18 Displaying DHCP Message Count

```
Router#show ip dhcp server statistics
```

If you would like to see information about addresses returned and allocated as well as address lease information, use the **debug ip dhcp server events** command, which is shown in Example 15-19.

Example 15-19 Displaying DHCP Processes

```
Router#debug ip dhcp server events
```

1.2.8—If you have a DHCP server in a different network and would like DHCP broadcasts to forward across a subnet on a router, you can use the **ip helper-address** command, as shown in Example 15-20. This command allows you to configure a router to forward the following services:

- Time

- Terminal Access Controller Access Control System (TACACS)

- Domain Name Service (DNS)

- Bootstrap Protocol (BOOTP)/DHCP Server

- BOOTP/DHCP Client

- Trivial File Transfer Protocol (TFTP)

- NetBIOS Name Service

- NetBIOS Datagram Service

Use the following command to forward a DHCP broadcast:

```
ip helper-address address
```

Example 15-20 Forwarding DHCP Broadcasts Across a Router

```
Router#ip helper-address 192.168.17.1
```

CCNA 4, Module 6

6.2.7—If you have a Simple Network Management Protocol (SNMP) server running on your network and you would like to enable SNMP on your router, you can use the following commands:

```
snmp-server community community-string {ro ¦ rw}
snmp-server location location
snmp-server community contact
```

Example 15-21 Enabling SNMP on a Router

```
Router(config)#snmp-server community campus3 ro
Router(config)#snmp-server location building1A
Router(config)#snmp-server contact Matt S. 555-1234
```

The **ro** and **rw** options stand for *read only* and *read write*.

Summary

Passwords for router access, DHCP, NAT, and PAT all provide additional functionality for your router. You can benefit greatly from the advantages of using internal private addressing from both an expense and security standpoint. You can review some of these concepts in pages 475–486 in the *CCNA Flash Cards and Exam Practice Pack* (CCNA Self-Study, exam #640-801), Second Edition.

Your Notes

Configure a Switch with VLANs and Interswitch Communication

Switches allow you to completely restructure your network design with a couple of keystrokes. Amazing. Virtual LANs (VLANs) and the VLAN Trunking Protocol (VTP) allow you to avoid the myriad ports and Category 5 cable that your hub-wielding predecessors battled during their attempts to segment and scale a network. Modules 8 and 9 from CCNA 3 explain the concepts and configurations behind VLANs and VTP. Today, you review the syntax for VLAN and VTP configuration commands and see examples of how the commands should look in the command-line interface (CLI). Consider today's information a primer for hands-on review in the lab or with a simulator.

CCNA 3, Module 8

8.2.1 and 8.2.2—VLANs allow you to logically separate a network into Layer 3 subnets. The flexibility of VLAN implementation provides the following features:

- VLAN membership based on job assignment regardless of location

- VLAN membership that follows the users when they change location on the network

- VLAN membership that provides security settings assigned for each logical group

You can configure switches to share VLAN information with frame tagging using Inter-Switch Link (ISL) or Institute of Electrical and Electronics Engineers (IEEE) 802.1Q. ISL is a Cisco proprietary protocol, while IEEE 802.1Q is an open standard. Although it is possible to assign VLANs based on job function, it is most common to assign VLANs based on geographic location, as corporations work to centralize network resources. A VLAN can be as small as a department or as large as an entire building.

8.2.3—You would configure static VLANs if your network design fits the following description:

- You have VLAN software to configure ports.

- You plan to control any and all moved workstations.

- You do not want to manage by MAC address.

The switch configured for static VLANs should also be in VTP server mode. You also need to adhere to the following requirements of VLAN 1:

- VLAN 1 is one of the factory default VLANs.

- VLAN 1 must be the default Ethernet VLAN.

- VLAN 1 must carry VLAN Trunking Protocol (VTP) and Cisco Discovery Protocol (CDP) traffic.

By default, the switch's IP address is in the VLAN1 broadcast domain.

The commands to create a static VLAN using the **vlan database** command and apply the VLAN to interfaces are as follows:

```
vlan database
vlan vlan-number
interface interface
switchport access vlan vlan-number
```

Example 14-1   Configuring a VLAN Using the vlan database Command

```
Switch#vlan database
Switch(vlan)#vlan 2
Switch(vlan)#exit
Switch#configure terminal
Switch(config)#interface fastethernet 0/4
Switch(config-if)#switchport mode access
Switch(config-if)#switchport access vlan 2
```

VLAN configuration is now preferred in global configuration mode rather than using the **vlan database** command. The commands to create a VLAN and apply the VLAN to interfaces in global configuration mode are as follows:

```
vlan vlan-number
interface interface
switchport mode access
switchport access vlan vlan-number
```

Example 14-2   Configuring a VLAN in Global Configuration Mode

```
Switch#configure terminal
Switch(config)#vlan 2
Switch(config-vlan)#exit
Switch(config)#interface fastethernet 0/4
Switch(config-if)#switchport mode access
Switch(config-if)#switchport access vlan 2
```

8.2.4—The following commands allow you to verify your VLAN configuration:

```
show vlan
show vlan brief
show vlan id {id ¦ name} vlan
```

Remember that all ports are in VLAN1 by default.

8.2.5—If you created your VLAN in global configuration mode, you can use the **show running config** and **show vlan** commands to capture VLAN configuration settings with the text capture feature in HyperTerminal. You can also back up your VLAN configuration with the following command:

```
copy running-config tftp
```

8.2.6—To remove a VLAN, you use the **no** statement at the beginning of the VLAN configuration command, as shown in Examples 14-3 and 14-4.

Example 14-3   Deleting a VLAN Using the vlan database Command

```
Switch#vlan database
Switch(vlan)#no vlan 2
Switch(vlan)#exit
```

Example 14-4   Deleting a VLAN in Global Configuration Mode

```
Switch#configure terminal
Switch(config)#no vlan 2
```

CCNA 3, Module 9

9.1.1–9.1.4—A trunk between switches is a physical and logical connection that passes network traffic. The trunk link provides a single backbone connection for multiple VLANs between switches. Trunking protocols allow switches to send information from multiple VLANs across a single channel. Two types of trunking protocols are frame filtering and frame tagging. The IEEE has defined frame tagging as the standard trunking type. As mentioned previously, the two types of frame tagging are the Cisco proprietary ISL and IEEE 802.1Q. A switch uses frame tagging to add header information to each frame identifying the VLAN ID of that frame for other switches connected through a trunk link.

9.1.5—The following command configures trunking on a Catalyst 2900 switch:

```
switchport trunk encapsulation {isl ¦ dot1q}
```

Example 14-5   Configuring VLAN Trunking on a 2900

```
Switch(config)#interface fastethernet 0/12
Switch(config-if)#switchport trunk vlan isl
```

On a Cisco Catalyst 2950, you do not need this command because 802.1Q is the only encapsulation available. To look at the type of trunking configured on a Catalyst 2900, use the following command:

```
show trunk module/port
```

Make sure that you use all the **show** commands in this book when you are practicing in a lab or simulation so that you are familiar with the output.

9.2.1–9.2.3—VTP allows you to manage your VLANs with Layer 2 trunk frames. You can add, delete, and rename VLANs using VTP. You can configure VLANs to be encapsulated in ISL or 802.1Q frames. VTP messages always contain the following items:

- VTP protocol version

- VTP message type

- Management domain length

- Management domain name

Table 14-1 outlines the three possible modes for a VTP switch.

Table 14-1   VTP Switch Modes

VTP Mode	Capabilities	Definition
Server	Can create, modify, and delete VLANs	Sends VTP messages out all trunk ports and saves VLAN configuration in the NVRAM.
Client	Cannot create, modify, and delete VLANs	Better for switches that do not have enough memory for large configurations. VTP clients process changes and forward messages.
Transparent	Only forwards advertisements	Forwards the messages, but does not modify its own independent VLAN database.

VLAN modifications occur only in the VTP domain where they originate. The configuration revision number of a VTP update determines whether or not a switch will overwrite its database. The switch overwrites its database information using the most recent update with the highest configuration revision number. VTP maintains its own NVRAM, and the configuration register can only be reset if you clear the NVRAM and reboot the switch. By default, VTP does not operate in secure mode.

9.2.4—Switches use VTP to multicast the following information:

- Management domain

- Configuration revision number

- Known VLANs

- Known VLAN parameters

Once you have set up a VTP domain, you need to configure only one device, and all the other devices learn from this device. VTP advertisements start with the configuration register number 0, increase by 1 until they reach 2,147,483,648, and then start again at 0. VTP advertisements are either a request from a client or a response from a server. The three types of VTP messages are as follows:

- **Advertisement requests**—Clients request VLAN information.

- **Summary advertisements**—The switch sends summary advertisements every five minutes. A switch updates its database only if the configuration revision number is higher than the switch's current revision number.

- **Subset advertisements**—Subset advertisements are triggered by changes to VLAN settings such as creation or deletion. These advertisements provide specific information about VLANs.

9.2.5—To set up VTP, you need to configure the version number, the VTP domain, the VTP mode, and a password with the following commands:

```
vlan database
vtp v2-mode
vtp domain domain
vtp {client ¦ server ¦ transparent}
vtp password password
```

Example 14-6   Configuring a VTP Server

```
Switch#vlan database
Switch(vlan)#vtp v2-mode
Switch(vlan)#vtp domain group3
Switch(vlan)#vtp server
Switch(vlan)#vtp password cisco
```

Once you have completed the VTP configuration, you can quickly check it with the following commands:

```
show vtp status
show vtp counters
```

9.3.2–9.3.6—You need to use a Layer 3 router in order to allow devices to communicate across VLANs. You can connect a physical router interface to each VLAN just as you would connect router interfaces to separate switches, or you can use one physical interface and configure logical subinterfaces for each VLAN. If your router has one 100 Mbps connection to a switch with VLANs 1, 20, and 30, you can configure the interface with the following commands for each subinterface:

```
interface fastethernet slot-number/port.subinterface-number
encapsulation dot1q vlan-number
ip address ip-address subnet-mask
```

Example 14-7   Router VLAN Subinterface Configuration

```
Router(config)#interface fastethernet 0/0.1
Router(config-if)#encapsulation dot1q 1
Router(config-if)#ip address 192.168.1.1 255.255.255.0
Router(config)#interface fastethernet 0/0.2
Router(config-if)#encapsulation dot1q 20
Router(config-if)#ip address 192.168.2.1 255.255.255.0
Router(config)#interface fastethernet 0/0.3
Router(config-if)#encapsulation dot1q 30
Router(config-if)#ip address 192.168.3.1 255.255.255.0
```

In Example 14-7, as always, VLAN1 is the management VLAN. It cannot be deleted and carries VTP and CDP.

Summary

Most switches work right out of those cool Cisco shipping boxes, but a true CCNA (or CCNA in training) would strive to implement the additional features available in a switch. You can divide the network logically with VLANs and then push that configuration across multiple switches with VTP. Another source for review of today's material can be found in pages 111–120 and 350–386 in the *CCNA Flash Cards and Exam Practice Pack* (CCNA Self-Study, exam #640-801), Second Edition.

Your Notes

Implement a LAN

Today's objective, implementing a LAN, seems about as easy to pin down for details as implementing world peace. However, this objective provides a good opportunity to talk about some LAN topics, such as bandwidth and cabling, that do not fit well elsewhere. Modules 2, 4, 5, and 7 from CCNA 1 provide information about LAN implementation.

CCNA 1, Module 2

2.2.1–2.2.7—Bandwidth represents the amount of data you can transfer over a network. LAN bandwidth is faster than WAN bandwidth, and you typically need to purchase bandwidth for your WAN connection. Table 13-1 displays the units you use to describe bandwidth.

Table 13-1   Bandwidth Units

Unit	Abbreviation	Comparison
Bits per second	bps	This is the base unit
Kilobits per second	kbps	1000 bits per second
Megabits per second	Mbps	1,000,000 bits per second
Gigabits per second	Gbps	10^9 bits per second
Terabits per second	Tbps	10^{12} bits per second

Category 5 (Cat 5) unshielded twisted pair (UTP) copper cabling is presently physically limited to 1 Gbps, but the devices and signaling type that you implement in a LAN determine the actual bandwidth. If you use 100 Mbps switches, your LAN will operate at 100 Mbps. Table 13-2 provides bandwidth specifications for devices, maximum bandwidth, and maximum distance.

Table 13-2   Bandwidth Units

Media Type	Bandwidth in Mbps	Maximum Distance
10Base2 Ethernet Thinnet, Coaxial	10	185 meters
10Base5 Ethernet Thicknet, Coaxial	10	500 meters
10BaseT Ethernet Category 5 UTP	10	100 meters
100BaseTX Ethernet Category 5 UTP	100	100 meters
1000BaseTX Ethernet Category 5 UTP	1000	100 meters
100BaseFX Ethernet Multimode Optical Fiber	100 or 1000	220 meters
1000BaseSX Ethernet Multimode Optical Fiber	1000	550 meters
1000BaseLX Ethernet Singlemode Optical Fiber	1000	5000 meters

The maximum bandwidth may be different from the actual throughput on your network. The type of data, devices, number of users, and power conditions can affect throughput. Pay keen attention to the use of *bits* in bandwidth measurement and not *bytes*. One byte is equal to eight bits. You typically use bytes and megabytes to describe file sizes. Do not confuse megabits per second with megabytes. It would take 8 seconds in perfect conditions to transfer 1 MB of data over a 1 Mbps connection.

CCNA 1, Module 4

4.2.1—Your network cabling will likely include one or many of the types of cable outlined in Table 13-3.

Table 13-3   Cable Types

Cable Type	Use	Features
Coaxial	Thicknet and Thinnet	Shielded, single copper wire, more expensive and difficult to install than UTP
Unshielded twisted pair (UTP)	Common network installation cable	No shielding, yet inexpensive and easy to install
Shielded twisted pair (STP)	Network installations where noise exists and fiber is less practical	IBM-specific cable with two conductors individually covered with grounded foil shielding inside of braided shielding for the entire cable
Screened twisted pair (ScTP)	Network installations where noise exists and fiber is less practical	Category 5 cable with grounded foil shielding, more expensive than UTP
Fiber-optic	Long-distance and/or high noise network installations	Not affected by electrical noise, capable of longer distances, more expensive than UTP

4.2.2—The following three terms define factors that can affect network signals:

- **Attenuation**—The decrease in the strength of a signal as it travels across physical media.

- **Impedance**—The resistance of the physical media that can cause a signal to attenuate. A bad connection or cable discontinuity can result in signal echoes causing signal jitter.

- **Insertion loss**—The combination of attenuation and impedance effect on a signal.

4.2.3–4.2.5—When you run cable for a LAN, it is important to consider sources of noise that can affect your signal. Noise can be any electrical source that distorts the signal on a cable. Noise that originates from other cables or wires is defined as crosstalk. Table 13-4 outlines different types of crosstalk.

Table 13-4   Noise

Type	Definition
Near-end crosstalk (NEXT)	Crosstalk from another wire pair on the same end of the link
Far-end crosstalk (FEXT)	Crosstalk on the far end of the link, less significant due to attenuation
Power sum near-end crosstalk (PSNEXT)	The effect of NEXT from all wire pairs in a cable

The TIA/EIA-568-B standard requires a cable to return acceptable levels for ten cable parameters including NEXT, FEXT, and PSNEXT.

CCNA 1, Module 5

5.1.5 and 5.2.7—Table 13-5 explains when you would use a crossover, straight-through, or rollover UTP cable.

Table 13-5   UTP Cabling for Network Devices

Cable	Used to Connect	Description
Crossover cable	Switch to switch	TIA/EIA-568-A on one end and TIA/EIA-568-B on the other end.
	Switch to hub	
	Hub to hub	
	Router to router	
	Host/server to host	
	Router to host	
Straight-through cable	Router to switch	TIA/EIA-568-A on both ends or TIA/EIA-568-B on both ends.
	Router to hub	
	Host/server to switch	
	Host/server to hub	
Rollover cable	Terminal to console port on a device for configuration, typically a serial port on a host to a console port on a router or switch	Pins 1–8 reversed on either end. Often converted to 9-pin serial on one end.

CCNA 1, Module 7

7.1.1–7.2.1—10Base5, 10Base2, and 10BaseT are legacy 10 Mbps Ethernet standards that you would likely replace with 100 Mbps 100BaseTX Fast Ethernet or 1000BaseTX Gigabit Ethernet. Remember that UTP copper cabling can run only 100 meters between devices. For longer cable standards, you would use 100BaseFX, 1000BaseSX, and 1000BaseLX.

Summary

UTP now rules the LAN in most situations. The type of cable you use dictates the distance and maximum bandwidth of your link. Remember that noise can render a network unusable and your data unreadable if you cable your LAN incorrectly. Combine your knowledge of switching and cabling to answer pages 52–92 in the *CCNA Flash Cards and Exam Practice Pack* (CCNA Self-Study, exam #640-801), Second Edition.

Your Notes

Customize a Switch Configuration to Meet Specified Requirements and Manage System Image and Device Configuration Files (Two Objectives)

Today and on Day 11 you cover two objectives in one day. The super short switch configuration customization objective fits nicely with the longer system image and configuration file management objective. Not to mention that "31 Days to the CCNA" sounds a lot better than "33 Days to the CCNA."

Customize a Switch Configuration to Meet Specified Requirements

Static and dynamic virtual LAN (VLAN) assignment, switching modes, Virtual Terminal Protocol (VTP), and subinterface configurations all provide the means to customize a switch configuration for your specific network requirements. You have covered the specifics of these concepts and configurations on Day 14, "Configure a Switch with VLANs and Interswitch Communication," and you will cover the initial configuration of a switch on Day 11, "Perform an Initial Configuration on a Router and Perform an Initial Configuration on a Switch (Two Objectives)." Today you focus on switch placement and layered model references found in Modules 4 and 5 from CCNA 3.

CCNA 3, Module 4

4.2.1–4.2.9 and 4.3.6—If you connect any number of computers to a hub, those computers all see each other and have to deny or accept every transmission that occurs on that network. You can divide this single collision domain with a switch and keep local traffic local because the switch filters based on the MAC address. The only time that all devices see a transmission is when a host needs to ask all other hosts for information in the form of a broadcast. Routers have enough network knowledge to respond to broadcasts for their connected segments and thus to filter broadcasts. When you implement a LAN, consider the following three points when placing and configuring network devices:

- Bridges and switches divide collision domains and filter at Layer 2. Each port on a bridge or switch is microsegmented into its own collision domain.

- Layer 2 switches can also divide broadcast domains with VLANs, but you need a router to communicate between VLANs.

- Layer 3 switches and routers filter at Layer 3 of the OSI model and divide broadcast domains.

CCNA 3, Module 5

5.2.1–5.2.6—Although there are beefy switches at the core layer of a network and Layer 3 switches at the distribution layer, you will spend most of your time configuring VLANs and VTP at the access layer of your network. How you want a user to connect to the distribution layer will determine the specific configuration of your switches.

Manage System Image and Device Configuration Files

After you configure your network and everything functions properly, it is a great idea to back up your configurations. As new security threats surface and new software features emerge, you will likely decide to upgrade your network device software. Modules 3 and 5 from CCNA 2 provide the information to accomplish these tasks.

CCNA 2, Module 3

3.2.8 and 3.2.9—You can store a configuration file on a TFTP server, a network server, or a disk. To save your router configuration to a TFTP server, make sure you know the IP address of the TFTP server and use the following command:

```
copy running-config tftp
{enter host IP address}
{type a name for the configuration file}
{type y}
```

Example 12-1   Back Up a Configuration to a TFTP Server

```
Router#copy running-config tftp
Remote host []?192.168.1.80
Name of configuration file to write [Router-config]?configbackup.1
Write the file configbackup.1 to 192.168.1.80 [confirm] y
Writing configbackup.1 !!!!!! [ok]
```

To restore the file to your router, use the following commands:

```
copy tftp running-config
{select a host or network configuration file}
{enter host IP address}
{type the name of the configuration file}
{type y}
```

Example 12-2   Restore a Backup Configuration from a TFTP Server

```
Router#copy tftp running-config
Address or name of remote host []? 192.168.1.80
Source filename []? Configbackup.1
Destination filename [running-config]? running-config
Accessing tftp://192.168.1.80/configbackup.1
!!!!!!!!!!!!!!!
752 bytes copied in 8.03 secs
Router#
```

You can also copy the output of the **show run** command from your terminal and paste it into a text file to back up a configuration.

CCNA 2, Module 5

5.1.1—A router starts using the following sequence:

1. The router checks the hardware (POST) and loads the bootstrap code from the read-only memory (ROM).

2. The router first looks for the Cisco IOS image in the flash memory, then looks for a TFTP server that could have the IOS image, and finally, if there is no other option, loads a stripped version of the IOS image from ROM.

3. Once the IOS image is loaded, the router first looks for a configuration file in the NVRAM, then looks for a TFTP server that might have the configuration, and lastly, if there is no configuration, outputs a set of questions to the console to ask the user for configuration parameters.

5.1.2 and 5.1.3—You can define where a router should look for the IOS by entering boot system commands in global configuration mode. The order in which you enter the commands will define the order in which the router will use them to find an IOS image. The purpose of these boot system commands is to override the router's default configuration register. The commands will be visible in the running-config and startup-config (if saved) and are only used when the register value is set (see Table 12-1).

```
boot system flash IOS-filename
boot system tftp IOS-filename tftp-address
boot system rom
```

Example 12-3   Boot System Commands

```
Router(config)#boot system flash myios-image
Router(config)#boot system tftp myios-image 192.168.1.80
Router(config)#boot system rom
Router(config)#exit
Router#copy running-config startup-config
```

5.1.4—You can also define how a router should boot by editing the configuration register in the NVRAM. The **show version** command will display the current settings, and the following command will allow you to change the configuration register:

```
config-register configuration-register-value
```

Example 12-4   Change the Configuration Register

```
Router(config)#config-register 0x2102
```

Table 12-1 displays the values and descriptions for the configuration register.

Table 12-1   Configuration Register Values

Register Value	Example	Description
0x___0	0x2100	System enters ROM monitor mode. Use **b** to boot the system.
0x___1	0x2101	Boots the first image in flash. This setting will boot the limited ROM version on older platforms.
0x___2 to 0x___F	0x2142	Looks in the NVRAM for boot system commands. If there are no commands, the system boots the first image in flash.

5.1.5—Use the following command to check the configuration register value and the boot image source:

```
show version
```

If you would like to check the boot system commands, use the following **show** command:

```
show running-config
```

5.2.1—Cisco IOS release 12.0 and later releases use the Cisco IOS File System (IFS). The IFS allows you to follow a single command convention to manage the file system. The parameters for an IFS management command are as follows:

```
copy location:URL location:URL
```

Example 12-5   Copy a Configuration File with TFTP Using IFS URL Conventions

```
Router#copy tftp://192.168.1.80/backup-config system:running-config
```

RAM, NVRAM, and flash hold the following configuration files:

- **Running configuration**—Contained in the RAM
- **Startup configuration**—Contained in the NVRAM
- **Cisco IOS image**—Contained in flash

5.2.2—Figure 12-1 provides an example for the IOS naming convention.

Figure 12-1   A Cisco IOS Name Example

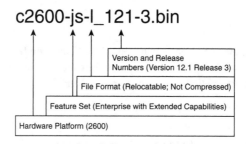

c2600-js-l_121-3.bin

Version and Release
Numbers (Version 12.1 Release 3)

File Format (Relocatable; Not Compressed)

Feature Set (Enterprise with Extended Capabilities)

Hardware Platform (2600)

5.2.5—The following commands back up a Cisco IOS image:

```
copy flash tftp
{enter the source filename}
{enter TFTP server IP address}
{enter or select the destination file name}
```

Example 12-6   Back Up a Cisco IOS Image to a TFTP Server

```
Router#copy flash tftp
Source filename []? c2600-is-mz
Address or name of remote host []?192.168.1.80
Destination filename [c2600-is-mz]? c2600-is-mz-jan06
```

The following command allows you to restore a Cisco IOS image:

```
copy tftp flash
{enter TFTP server IP address}
{enter the source filename}
{enter or select the destination file name}
```

Example 12-7   Restore an IOS Image from a TFTP Server

```
Router#copy tftp flash
Address or name of remote host []?192.168.1.80
Source filename []? c2600-is-mz-jan06
Destination filename [c2600-is-mz]? c2600-is-mz
```

5.2.6—If your router has a corrupted or missing IOS, you can use ROM monitor (ROMMON) mode to restore the image. You should first use the following ROMMON commands to check your Cisco IOS image file and ensure proper boot settings:

```
dir flash:
boot flash: image-name
```

If there is in fact an image in the flash and it boots properly with the ROMMON **boot flash** command, you should check your configuration register and boot system commands with these two **show** commands:

```
show version
show startup-config
```

If you do need to restore the image, you can use ROMMON and **xmodem** to copy the IOS through the console connection. In ROMMON mode, first use the **confreg** command to check your connection settings and then use the following **xmodem** command:

```
xmodem -c image-file-name
```

Example 12-8   Restore a Cisco IOS Image Using xmodem

```
rommon 2>xmodem -c c2600-is-mz.bin
```

Once your router is ready to receive, you will need to use your terminal program (HyperTerminal) to send the image that you have saved on your computer.

5.2.7—You can also use ROMMON to restore an image from TFTP using the **set** command to view your connection variables and then the **tftpdnld** command to restore the image:

```
set
tftpdnld
```

Example 12-9   Restore a Cisco IOS Image Using tftpdnld

```
rommon 1>set
IP_ADDRESS=192.168.1.10
IP_SUBNET_MASK=255.255.255.0
DEFAULT_GATEWAY=192.168.1.1
TFTP_SERVER=192.168.1.80
TFTP_FILE=/jan06/c2600-is-mz.bin
rommon 2>tftpdnld
```

If the **set** command displays incorrect variables, you can set the variables by entering the variable name followed by an = and then the desired setting. The variables and the filename are case sensitive.

5.2.8—You can check the current Cisco IOS image and amount of flash on a router with the **show version** command. The **show flash** command also shows the image and available flash in the router file system.

Summary

From the layered design to the exact configuration of each port, you will encounter numerous switching challenges. The software abilities of switches to reconstruct and organize traffic flow provide you with the tools to face such custom challenges. Pages 350–386 in the *CCNA Flash Cards and Exam Practice Pack* (CCNA Self-Study, exam #640-801), Second Edition, might help you to check your knowledge of switch configuration customization.

Proper configuration and organized Cisco IOS image management are a sign of a prepared network engineer. These commands come in handy when you set up your systems and then again when a system has problems. Pages 259–274 of the *CCNA Flash Cards and Exam Practice Pack* (CCNA Self-Study, exam #640-801), Second Edition, review these topics.

Your Notes

Perform an Initial Configuration on a Router and Perform an Initial Configuration on a Switch (Two Objectives)

Today, as on Day 12, you cover two objectives in one day. The initial configuration of a router and initial configuration of a switch represent the common tasks that you will perform when you take a Cisco networking device out of its box and add it to your network.

Perform an Initial Configuration on a Router

Day 11 provides a quick overview of the housekeeping commands required to organize and begin setup on routers and switches. Initial router configuration is spread throughout the curriculum, but Modules 2 and 3 from CCNA 2 focus on the key points necessary.

CCNA 2, Module 2

2.2.5—When you initially log in to a router, the first command mode you enter is user EXEC mode. User EXEC mode allows you to execute commands that show the status of a router. You can type **enable** to enter privileged EXEC mode, and the command prompt will change to a number symbol (#). The command **configure terminal** from privileged EXEC mode enters you into global configuration mode. From global configuration mode, you can enter a number of interface and specific configuration modes. Typing the command **exit** takes you back one mode at a time, whereas typing **end** or using the key combination **Ctrl-Z** places you back at the privileged EXEC mode.

2.2.6 and 2.2.7—While logged in to the router, you can use the question mark (?) to see a list of available commands. If the output is more than a page, pressing the **Spacebar** enables you to view the next screen. You can also type a command followed by a question mark (?) to see possible ways to complete the command. The **clock** command is a great way to try out the question mark (?). If there is an error in a command, the caret symbol (^) will note where the command may have an error. A dollar symbol ($) at the beginning of a long line indicates that the line has been scrolled to the left. Table 11-1 displays the editing commands that you may sometimes use and that you will always need to know for the CCNA exam.

Table 11-1   Cisco IOS Editing Keys and Commands

Keystroke or Command	Definition
Tab	Automatically complete a command
Ctrl-P or Up Arrow	Repeat previously typed command
Ctrl-A	Move to the beginning of a command line
Esc-B	Move back one word
Ctrl-B or Left Arrow	Move back one character
Ctrl-E	Move to the end of the command line
Ctrl-F or Right Arrow	Move forward one character
Esc-F	Move forward one word
Ctrl-Z	Exit configuration mode
terminal no editing	Turn off advanced editing mode

2.2.8—Table 11-2 displays the keys and commands related to the Cisco IOS command history.

Table 11-2   Cisco IOS Command History Keys and Commands

Keystroke or Command	Definition
Ctrl-P or Up Arrow	Repeat the last command
Ctrl-N or Down Arrow	Repeat the most recent command in the history buffer
show history	Display the command buffer
terminal history size *number*	Set the history buffer size
terminal no editing	Turn off advanced editing
terminal editing	Enable advanced editing

CCNA 2, Module 3

3.1.1–3.2.7—Example 11-1 shows a sample initial configuration on a router (does not include a routing protocol).

Example 11-1   Router Initial Configuration Example

```
Router>enable
Router#configure terminal
Router(config)#hostname RouterA
RouterA(config)#banner motd #
Enter TEXT message. End with the character '#'.
Welcome to RouterA
#
RouterA(config)#enable secret class
RouterA(config)#line console 0
RouterA(config-line)#password cisco
RouterA(config-line)#login
RouterA(config-line)#exit
RouterA(config)#line vty 0 4
RouterA(config-line)#password cisco
RouterA(config-line)#login
RouterA(config-line)#exit
RouterA(config)#interface fa0/0
RouterA(config-if)#ip address 192.168.1.1 255.255.255.0
RouterA(config-if)#description Main Office LAN
RouterA(config-if)#no shutdown
RouterA(config-if)#no shutdown
RouterA(config-if)#exit
RouterA(config)#ip host RouterA 192.168.1.1
RouterA(config)#exit
RouterA#copy running-config startup-config
```

Perform an Initial Configuration on a Switch

Many switches work perfectly on a small network without any additional configuration. You can, however, add both security and better organization to your network by completing the initial configuration of a switch, covered in Module 6 from CCNA 3.

CCNA 3, Module 6

6.2.1 and 6.2.2—By default, a switch has only VLAN 1 and no IP address. VLAN 1 is also called the *management VLAN*. You can assign an IP address to a virtual interface in VLAN 1 for remote management. To completely clear a switch, use the following commands:

```
delete flash:vlan.dat
erase startup-config
reload
```

Example 11-2   Clearing a Switch Configuration

```
Switch#delete flash:vlan.dat
Switch#erase startup-config
Switch#reload
```

Example 11-3 provides the commands to implement a basic switch configuration on a Catalyst 2950.

Example 11-3   A Basic Switch Configuration on a Catalyst 2950

```
Switch>enable
Switch#configure terminal
Switch(config)#hostname SwitchA
SwitchA(config)#line con 0
SwitchA(config-line)#password cisco
SwitchA(config-line)#login
SwitchA(config-line)#line vty 0 15
SwitchA(config-line)#password cisco
SwitchA(config-line)#login
SwitchA(config-line)#exit

SwitchA(config)#enable secret class
SwitchA(config)#interface VLAN 1
SwitchA(config-if)#ip address 192.168.1.2 255.255.255.0
SwitchA(config-if)#no shutdown
SwitchA(config-if)#exit
SwitchA(config)#ip default-gateway 192.168.1.1
SwitchA(config)#copy running-config startup-config
```

Example 11-4 provides the commands to implement a basic switch configuration on a Catalyst 1900.

Example 11-4   A Basic Switch Configuration on a Catalyst 1900

```
Switch>enable
Switch#configure terminal
Switch(config)#hostname SwitchA
SwitchA(config)#enable secret class
SwitchA(config)#ip address 192.168.1.2 255.255.255.0
SwitchA(config)#ip default-gateway 192.168.1.1
```

6.2.3—A switch maintains a MAC address table that you can view and clear with the following commands:

```
show mac-address table
clear mac-address table
```

6.2.4—The following command assigns a static MAC address to a port on a switch:

```
mac-address-table static host-mac-address interface interface vlan vlan
```

Example 11-5   Static MAC Address Configuration

```
Switch(config)#mac-address-table static 0011.2233.4455 interface FastEthernet 0/3
vlan 1
```

Use the command **no** in front of Example 11-5 to remove the static MAC address configuration.

6.2.5—If you are concerned about users attempting to falsify Layer 2 information (MAC spoofing) on your network, you can allow only one MAC address to be used per port with the following commands to enable port security:

```
switchport mode access
switchport port-security
switchport port-security maximum {maximum-number-of-MACs-per-port}
switchport port-security violation {restrict ¦ shutdown}
```

Example 11-6   Port Security Configuration

```
Switch(config)#interface fastethernet 0/2
Switch(config-if)#switchport mode access
Switch(config-if)#switchport port-security
Switch(config-if)#switchport port-security maximum 1
Switch(config-if)#switchport port-security violation shutdown
```

Port security is a good alternative to managing all MAC addresses on a network with static configuration unless you have no scruples and you are getting paid by the hour.

6.2.6 and 6.2.7—Make sure that any new switch you are adding to a network has a basic configuration similar to the ones in section 6.2.2 of the CCNA 3 course. You should also be able to move the switch operating system to a TFTP server as a backup. The commands in Example 11-7 allow you to back up your switch operating system on a Cisco Catalyst 2950 switch.

**Example 11-7   Back Up the Switch Software to a TFTP Server on a Cisco Catalyst 2950
Switch**

```
Switch#copy flash tftp
Source filename []? c2950-i6q4l2-mz.121-13.EA1.bin
Address or name of remote host []? 192.168.1.80
Destination filename [c2950-i6q4l2-mz.121-13.EA1.bin]? c2950-i6q4l2-mz.121-13.EA1-
jan06.bin
```

The commands in Example 11-8 allow you to back up your switch operating system on a Cisco Catalyst 2900 switch.

Example 11-8   Back Up the Switch Software to a TFTP Server on a Cisco Catalyst 2900 Switch

```
Switch#copy flash:c2950-i6q4l2-mz.121-13.EA1.bin tftp
Source filename [c2950-i6q4l2-mz.121-13.EA1.bin]? [press enter]
Destination IP address or hostname []? 192.168.1.80
Destination filename [c2950-i6q4l2-mz.121-13.EA1.bin]? c2950-i6q4l2-mz.121-13.EA1-jan06.bin
```

Use the commands shown in Example 11-9 to restore the switch operating system.

Example 11-9   Restore the Switch Software from a TFTP Server on a Cisco Catalyst 2950 or 2900 Switch

```
Switch#copy tftp flash
Address or name of remote host []? 192.168.1.80
Source filename []? c2950-i6q4l2-mz.121-13.EA1.bin
Destination filename [c2950-i6q4l2-mz.121-13.EA1.bin]? [press enter]
```

A Catalyst 1900 switch requires you to use the configuration menu to download a new software image to your switch. The Catalyst 1900 is not able to upload an image.

Summary

Configuring a hostname and initial passwords on a router should be as common to you as washing the dishes. The initial setup of a router provides you with a quick warm-up for the advanced commands that are not as intuitive. You can also quiz yourself with pages 211–238 from the *CCNA Flash Cards and Exam Practice Pack* (CCNA Self-Study, exam #640-801), Second Edition.

Today, you also covered slightly more than the initial configuration of a switch. Once you have skimmed through the process to add passwords, hostnames, and addressing to a switch, you should practice on a simulator or in a lab on different models. You can also get a quick quiz fix from the *CCNA Flash Cards and Exam Practice Pack* (CCNA Self-Study, exam #640-801), Second Edition, pages 205–210.

Your Notes

Implement an Access List

Ten days to the exam. For this final countdown to the CCNA, you will encounter short chapters that will allow you to review quickly and still have time for hands-on practice and practice exams.

Today provides the third installment of the access control list (ACL) quartet in this book. Day 25, "Evaluate Rules for Packet Control," and Day 19, "Develop an Access List to Meet User Specifications," discussed ACL design and theory. Today you review ACL configuration, and Day 3, "Troubleshoot an Access List," briefly covers ACL troubleshooting. All of these days review the information covered in Module 11 of CCNA 2.

CCNA 2, Module 11

11.1.3—Table 10-1 defines the range of numbers that you can use to define ACLs.

Table 10-1   Access Control List Number Specifications

Protocol	Range
Standard IP	1–99, 1300–1999
Extended IP	100–199, 2000–2699
AppleTalk	600–699
IPX	800–899
Extended IPX	900–999
IPX Service Advertising Protocol	1000–1099

You use the following commands to configure a standard access list and then to apply that access list to an interface:

```
access-list ACL-number {deny ¦ permit} source-address wildcard-mask
ip access-group ACL-number {in ¦ out}
```

Example 10-1   Standard Access Control List

```
Router(config)#access-list 25 deny 192.168.1.0 0.0.0.255
Router(config)#access-list 25 permit any
Router(config)#int fa0/0
Router(config-if)#ip access-group 25 in
```

The term **any** represents a source of 0.0.0.0 and source-wildcard of 255.255.255.255. You should also keep in mind that a default **deny any** exists at the end of all access lists. You can only assign *one access list per protocol per direction per interface.* You can use the following commands to configure an extended access list.

```
access-list ACL-number {deny | permit} protocol source wildcard-mask
    destination wildcard-mask
ip access-group ACL-number {in | out}
```

Example 10-2   Extended Access Control List

```
Router(config)#access-list 101 deny tcp 192.168.1.0 0.0.0.255
   192.168.5.0 0.0.0.255
Router(config)#access-list 101 permit tcp any any
Router(config)#int fa0/0
Router(config-if)#ip access-group 101 in
```

11.2.1–11.2.3—While standard access lists filter only the source IP address, an extended ACL can filter the source address, destination address, and the Layer 4 protocol. The following examples of extended ACLs display these additional filtering options:

```
access-list ACL-number {deny | permit} protocol source wildcard destination
    wildcard operator port
ip access-group ACL-number {in | out}
```

Example 10-3   Extended Access Control List Filtering a Web Server

```
Router(config)#access-list 101 deny tcp any host 192.168.1.23 eq www
Router(config)#access-list 101 permit tcp any any
Router(config)#int fa0/0
Router(config-if)#ip access-group 101 in
```

The term **host** in an access list substitutes the wildcard mask 0.0.0.0 to match just one address. In Example 10-3, you can use **www** or the port number **80** to represent the Layer 4 HTTP protocol.

A named access list allows you to configure an alphanumeric name for an ACL and bypass the limits of numbering. The following commands allow you to configure a named ACL:

```
access-list {extended | standard} name
{deny | permit} protocol source wildcard destination wildcard operator port
ip access-group acl-name {in | out}
```

Example 10-4   Named Access Control List Filtering a Web Server

```
Router(config)#access-list extended filterweb
Router(config-ext-nacl)#deny tcp any host 192.168.1.23 eq www
Router(config-ext-nacl)#permit tcp any any
Router(config-ext-nacl)#exit
Router(config)#int fa0/0
Router(config-if)#ip access-group filterweb in
```

11.2.4—As a quick reminder from Day 25, remember to put an extended ACL as close to the source of the traffic you are filtering as possible. You should put a standard ACL as close to the destination of the traffic you are filtering as possible.

11.2.6—You can restrict vty access using access lists. You should apply the same restrictions to all vty lines. The **access-class** command replaces the **access-group** command when configuring access lists for vty lines. The following commands allow you to restrict vty access:

```
access-list ACL-number {deny ¦ permit} source-address wildcard-mask
access-class ACL-number {in ¦ out}
```

Example 10-5   Restrict vty with an Access Control List

```
Router(config)#access-list 5 permit host 192.168.1.30
Router(config)#line vty 0 4
Router(config-line)#access-class 5 in
```

Summary

To truly perform well on the access list portion of the CCNA exam, you need to design, document, implement, and troubleshoot ACLs on a functioning or simulated network. Spend some time in the Cisco IOS software at your lab or with a simulator to memorize the commands covered in this chapter. It would also help to read through pages 456–476 in the *CCNA Flash Cards and Exam Practice Pack* (CCNA Self-Study, exam #640-801), Second Edition.

Your Notes

Implement Simple WAN Protocols

On Day 24, "Evaluate Key Characteristics of WANs," and Day 19, "Develop an Access List to Meet User Specifications," you evaluated and selected routing protocols. Today you review the configurations of the WAN technologies Point-to-Point Protocol (PPP), Integrated Services Digital Network (ISDN), dial-on-demand routing (DDR), and Frame Relay. Module 1 from CCNA 2 and Modules 3, 4, and 5 from CCNA 4 discuss WAN protocol configuration.

CCNA 2, Module 1

1.1.4—On a LAN, routers choose the best path for Layer 3 packets across a network. On a WAN, routers also function at Layer 3 to direct packets, but they act as WAN devices as well and can require additional configuration to facilitate WAN connectivity.

CCNA 4, Module 3

3.3.1 and 3.3.2—You can configure authentication, compression, error detection, and multilink features in PPP. The following commands enable PPP encapsulation and configure compression, link quality, and load balancing:

```
encapsulation ppp
compress {predictor | stac}
ppp quality {1 to 100 as a percentage}
ppp multilink
```

Example 9-1   Enabling PPP

```
Router(config)#interface serial 0/0
Router(config-if)#encapsulation ppp
Router(config-if)#compress predictor
Router(config-if)#ppp quality 50
Router(config-if)#ppp multilink
```

3.3.3—Use the following commands to set up PPP authentication:

```
username name password secret-password
encapsulation ppp
ppp authentication {chap | chap pap | pap chap | pap}
ppp pap sent-username username password password
```

Example 9-2   PPP Authentication

```
Router(config)#username cisco password class
Router(config)#interface serial 0/0
Router(config-if)#encapsulation ppp
Router(config-if)#ppp authentication chap pap
Router(config-if)#ppp pap sent-username cisco password class
```

3.3.4—You can verify the PPP encapsulation configuration with the following command:

```
show interfaces
show interfaces serial
```

CCNA 4, Module 4

4.2.1—You can configure ISDN to use the same switch type for all interfaces on the router, or you can specify the switch type for specific interfaces. The following commands will configure ISDN to use the same switch type for all interfaces using BRI:

```
isdn switch-type switch-type
isdn spid{number} spid-number local-dial-number
encapsulation ppp
```

Example 9-3   ISDN BRI Configuration

```
Router(config)#isdn switch-type basic-ni
Router(config)#interface bri0/0
Router(config-if)#isdn spid1 51086750000001 8675000
Router(config-if)#isdn spid2 51086750010001 8675001
```

4.2.2—To configure ISDN PRI, you specify the switch type as well as the controller, framing type, line coding, group timeslot, and speed. The following commands allow you to set these parameters for an ISDN PRI T1:

```
controller t1
framing {sf | esf}
linecode {ami | b8zs | hdb3}
pri-group timeslots range
interface serial {slot/port: | unit:} {23 | 15}
isdn switch-type switch-type
```

Example 9-4   ISDN PRI T1 Configuration

```
Router(config)#controller t1 1/0
Router(config-controller)#framing esf
Router(config-controller)#linecode b8zs
Router(config-controller)#pri-group timeslots 1-24
Router(config-controller)#interface serial3/0:23
Router(config-if)#isdn switch-type primary-5ess
Router(config-if)#no cdp enable
```

You would use the following commands to configure an ISDN PRI E1:

```
controller e1
framing {crc4 | no-crc4}
linecode {ami | b8zs | hdb3}
pri-group timeslots range
interface serial {slot/port: | unit:} {23 | 15}
isdn switch-type switch-type
```

Example 9-5   ISDN PRI E1 Configuration

```
Router(config)#controller e1 1/0
Router(config-controller)#framing crc4
Router(config-controller)#linecode hdb3
Router(config-controller)#pri-group timeslots 1-31
Router(config-controller)#interface serial3/0:15
Router(config-if)#isdn switch-type primary-net5
Router(config-if)#no cdp enable
```

4.2.3—The following commands allow you to verify your ISDN configuration:

```
show isdn status
show isdn active
show dialer
show interface
```

4.3.1—Dial-on-demand routing (DDR) defines interesting traffic as network activity that causes a router to connect to a network. You can define a dialer-list on a Cisco router that tells the router what traffic should cause it to bring up a DDR link. DDR configurations do not filter traffic. If the link comes up due to interesting traffic, all traffic can pass over the link while it is active.

4.3.2–4.3.5—To configure DDR, you need to use static routes to lower the cost of the route. Access lists can also help you to better define interesting traffic. You would use the following commands to create a basic configuration for legacy DDR including a static route, an access list, and PPP configuration:

```
dialer-list number protocol protocol {permit | deny | list [access-list-number]}
interface interface
```

```
dialer-group number
dialer idle-timeout seconds-after-last-traffic
dialer map ip next-hop name next-hop-hostname dial-number
```

Example 9-6   Legacy DDR Configuration Without Access Lists

```
RouterA(config)#ip route 192.168.3.0 255.255.255.0 192.168.1.2
RouterA(config)#dialer-list 1 protocol ip permit
RouterA(config)#username RouterB password class
RouterA(config)#interface bri0/0
RouterA(config-if)#dialer-group 1
RouterA(config-if)#encapsulation ppp
RouterA(config-if)#ppp authentication chap
RouterA(config-if)#dialer idle-timeout 180
RouterA(config-if)#dialer map 192.168.1.1 name RouterB 8675309
```

Example 9-7   Legacy DDR Configuration with Access Lists

```
RouterA(config)#ip route 192.168.3.0 255.255.255.0 192.168.1.2
RouterA(config)#dialer-list 1 protocol ip list 101
RouterA(config)#access-list 101 deny tcp any any eq ftp
RouterA(config)#access-list 101 deny tcp any any eq telnet
RouterA(config)#access-list 101 permit ip any any
RouterA(config)#username RouterB password class
RouterA(config)#interface bri0/0
RouterA(config-if)#dialer-group 1
RouterA(config-if)#encapsulation ppp
RouterA(config-if)#ppp authentication chap
RouterA(config-if)#dialer idle-timeout 180
RouterA(config-if)#dialer map 192.168.1.1 name RouterB 8675309
```

4.3.6 and 4.3.7—Legacy DDR applies the configuration to a specific interface. If you use dialer profiles with DDR, router interfaces can apply the configuration on a per-call basis. With dialer profiles, you can do the following:

- Use different encapsulations and access lists

- Set minimum and maximum calls

- Enable and disable features

You can add configurations to virtual dialer interfaces and then apply them to a pool of physical interfaces. The following commands allow you to configure dialer profiles:

```
dialer-list number protocol protocol {permit ¦ deny ¦ list [access-list-number]}
interface dialer virtual-interface-number
dialer-group number
dialer remote name next-hop-hostname
```

```
dialer string dial-number
dialer-pool number
dialer idle-timeout seconds-after-last-traffic
dialer pool-member number priority priority
```

Example 9-8   DDR Profile Configuration Without Access Lists

```
RouterA(config)#ip route 192.168.3.0 255.255.255.0 192.168.1.2
RouterA(config)#dialer-list 1 protocol ip permit
RouterA(config)#username RouterB password class
RouterA(config)#interface dialer 0
RouterA(config-if)#ip address 192.168.1.1 255.255.255.0
RouterA(config-if)#dialer-group 1
RouterA(config-if)#dialer remote name RouterB
RouterA(config-if)#dialer string 8675309
RouterA(config-if)#dialer pool 1
RouterA(config-if)#interface bri0/0
RouterA(config-if)#encapsulation ppp
RouterA(config-if)#ppp authentication chap
RouterA(config-if)#dialer idle-timeout 180
RouterA(config-if)#dialer pool-member 1 priority 50
```

4.3.8—The following commands allow you to verify your DDR configuration:

```
show dialer
show isdn active
show isdn status
```

CCNA 4, Module 5

5.2.1–**5.2.5**—You can configure your router for Frame Relay on a serial interface, and the default encapsulation type is Cisco HDLC. Although many non Cisco routers support this encapsulation, you can also use the Internet Engineering Task Force (IETF) standard encapsulation. The following commands configure a basic Frame Relay permanent virtual circuit (PVC):

```
encapsulation frame-relay {cisco | ietf}
frame-relay map protocol protocol-address dlci broadcast
```

Example 9-9 DTE Frame Relay PVC Configuration Without a Frame Relay Switch (No Local Management Interface [LMI])

```
RouterA(config)#interface serial 0
RouterA(config-if)#encapsulation frame-relay ietf
RouterA(config-if)#ip address 192.168.0.1 255.255.255.0
RouterA(config-if)#no shutdown
RouterA(config-if)#no keepalive
RouterA(config-if)#frame-relay map ip 192.168.0.2 151 ietf broadcast
RouterA(config-if)#description PVC to Portland, DLCI 151
```

For multiple connections across a Frame Relay network, you can configure subinterfaces. The subinterfaces can exist in their own subnet as *point-to-point* links, or you can configure the subinterfaces to share a single subnet as *multipoint* links. The following example shows a Frame Relay configuration with subinterfaces:

```
encapsulation frame-relay {cisco ¦ ietf}
frame-relay lmi-type {ansi ¦ cisco ¦ q933a}
interface serial {subinterface-number} {point-to-point ¦ multipoint}
frame-relay interface-dlci DLCI-number
```

Example 9-10 Frame Relay Configuration with Subinterfaces

```
RouterA(config)#interface serial 0
RouterA(config-if)#encapsulation frame-relay ietf
RouterA(config-if)#frame-relay lmi-type ansi
RouterA(config-if)#no shutdown
RouterA(config-if)#interface serial 0.130 point-to-point
RouterA(config-if)#description PVC to Boise, DLCI 130
RouterA(config-if)#ip address 192.168.1.1 255.255.255.0
RouterA(config-if)#frame-relay interface-dlci 130
RouterA(config-if)#interface serial 0.131 point-to-point
RouterA(config-if)#description PVC to Seattle, DLCI 131
RouterA(config-if)#ip address 192.168.2.1 255.255.255.0
RouterA(config-if)#frame-relay interface-dlci 131
```

5.2.6—The following commands allow you to verify your Frame Relay configuration:

```
show interfaces
show frame-relay lmi
show frame-relay pvc dlci-number
show frame-relay map
```

Summary

Although it is more difficult to find hands-on practice for WAN configurations, it is a good idea to at least work through simulations and practice the commands for the CCNA exam. PPP, ISDN, DDR, and Frame Relay configurations allow you to create complete networks that can span wide geographic areas. You can also quickly test your knowledge with pages 511–574 in the *CCNA Flash Cards and Exam Practice Pack* (CCNA Self-Study, exam #640-801), Second Edition.

Your Notes

Part IV

8–1 Day(s) Before the Exam—
Troubleshooting

Utilize the OSI Model as a Guide for Systematic Troubleshooting

The OSI seven-layer model allows you to chew a network into smaller, more digestible chunks. This division also provides a great framework for troubleshooting. OSI model–related troubleshooting is discussed in Module 2 from CCNA 1; Modules 8, 9, and 10 from CCNA 2; and Module 6 from CCNA 4.

CCNA 1, Module 2

2.3.3—Table 8-1 provides a quick review of the OSI seven-layer model.

Table 8-1   The Open System Interconnection Seven-Layer Model

Layer Number	Layer Name	Protocol Data Unit	Devices
7	Application	Data	N/A
6	Presentation	Data	N/A
5	Session	Data	N/A
4	Transport	Segment	N/A
3	Network	Packet	Router
2	Data link	Frame	Bridge, Switch
1	Physical	Bit	Hub, Repeater

CCNA 2, Module 8

8.1.5—You can test connectivity at OSI Layer 3 with the **ping** command. The **ping** command issues an Internet Control Message Protocol (ICMP) echo request and then receives an echo reply to verify connectivity. You typically issue the **ping** command followed by the IP address of the destination device.

CCNA 2, Module 9

9.2.1—The OSI model provides an excellent structure for network troubleshooting. You can begin at Layer 1 and work up to Layer 7 until you discover, solve, and document the issue.

9.2.2—The following steps outline a typical troubleshooting model:

Step 1   Collect information and analyze the symptoms of the problem.

Step 2   Localize the problem to a segment of the network, device, or user.

Step 3   Isolate the problem to a specific piece of hardware or software.

Step 4   Correct the problem.

Step 5   Verify that the problem has been corrected.

Step 6   Document the problem.

Steps 2 through 4 can be incorporated with the OSI model by checking, fixing, and verifying each layer, starting with Layer 1.

9.2.3–9.2.5—Problems at the first three layers of the OSI model are characterized by the following issues:

- **Physical layer (1)**—Problems with cables and power. Cables in the wrong port, improperly attached cables, and incorrect cable types are Layer 1 issues. Data terminal equipment (DTE) and data communications equipment (DCE) cable problems or transceiver issues also qualify as Layer 1 problems. Check all indicator LEDs and power LEDs before any other troubleshooting.

- **Data link layer (2)**—Improper or missing configurations for clock rate and encapsulation classify as Layer 2 issues. Serial and Ethernet configuration issues occur at Layer 2. Problems with a NIC can also be considered Layer 2 issues.

- **Network layer (3)**—IP addressing and routing protocol configuration issues occur at Layer 3. Incorrect subnet masks also classify as Layer 3 issues. Problems identified with the **ping** command (after testing Layers 1 and 2) are often Layer 3 issues. If you ping another device and receive the ICMP destination unreachable message, the packet was not delivered. You can use an extended ping command by typing **ping** without an IP address or hostname.

9.2.5—Telnet tests all seven layers of the OSI model. If you have a password configured for a vty on your routers and you can telnet between them, all seven layers of the OSI model function on your network. If you can ping a router but you cannot telnet to the router, you should first check your vty setup.

9.2.6—If you issue the **show interfaces** command, Layer 1 issues are indicated by the line status. If a router responds that the interface is down, it indicates that there is an issue with the cable or a connected device.

9.3.1–9.3.3—The **show interfaces** command can also provide you with information about Layer 2 problems. If the **show interface** command for a serial interface returns that the serial 0/0 is administratively down, you have not enabled the interface. A message that the interface is up but the line protocol is down indicates a Layer 2 issue, such as keepalives on the link or improper encapsulation. To verify connectivity at Layer 2 with Cisco devices, you can also use Cisco Discovery Protocol (CDP). You review CDP on Day 7, "Perform LAN and VLAN Troubleshooting."

CCNA 2, Module 10

10.1.3—A less obvious connectivity issue can occur at Layer 4 of the OSI model. The three-way handshake that occurs at the transport layer is susceptible to a denial of service (DoS) attack carried out with continuous synchronization flooding. You can use software to monitor and detect DoS attacks.

CCNA 4, Module 6

6.2.2 and 6.2.4—The OSI group also directed the development of a network management model. This model deals with network management applications that operate at the transport and application layers and often use Simple Network Management Protocol (SNMP) on Layer 4 port 161 and 162 User Datagram Protocol (UDP). The network information gathered by a management information base (MIB) can provide valuable network statistics for troubleshooting and recognizing issues with OSI Layers 4 through 7.

Summary

A clear understanding of the seven layers of the OSI model aids your ability to describe a network and to describe, document, and fix network issues. Although you covered them on Day 30, "Describe the Spanning Tree Process," it might not be a bad idea to return to pages 13–34 of the *CCNA Flash Cards and Exam Practice Pack* (CCNA Self-Study, exam #640-801), Second Edition for some good old OSI review.

Your Notes

Perform LAN and VLAN Troubleshooting

Cisco Discovery Protocol (CDP) is a great troubleshooting tool with Cisco devices. CDP gives you that extra layer of troubleshooting when **ping** and **telnet** yield unsatisfactory results. The Cisco Networking Academy Program covers methods for troubleshooting LANs and VLANs in Modules 4, 5, and 9 from CCNA 2 and Module 8 from CCNA 3.

CCNA 2, Module 4

4.1.1—All Cisco devices have CDP turned on by default. This makes your job a little easier when troubleshooting connectivity issues. CDP uses the Subnetwork Access Protocol (SNAP) to communicate over a network with directly connected neighbors. CDP is media and protocol independent and operates at the data link layer of the OSI model. This means you can properly connect and power up two Cisco devices and expect that they will exchange CDP advertisements over Layer 2 once you have enabled the interfaces with the **no shutdown** command and configured a clock rate for interfaces with a data communications equipment (DCE) cable attached. CDP version 2 (CDPv2) is the protocol running on devices with Cisco IOS Software Release 12.0(3)T or later.

4.1.2—The **show cdp neighbors** command reveals the following information about directly connected neighboring Cisco devices:

- Device ID
- Local interface
- Holdtime
- Capacity
- Platform

4.1.3 and 4.1.4—If you enter the command **cdp run** at the privileged EXEC prompt, you enable CDP on all interfaces on a device. If you enter into interface configuration mode, you can use the command **cdp enable** to start CDP on a specific interface. The command **clear cdp counters** clears gathered CDP information.

It is important to remember that the **show cdp** command shows information about the protocol only and that **show cdp neighbors** reveals information about connected devices. The following commands will display information about CDP and CDP-enabled devices:

```
show cdp traffic
show cdp
show cdp neighbors
show cdp neighbors detail
```

You can use the **show cdp neighbors detail** command to reveal the most information, including Layer 3 configurations of neighboring devices.

4.1.5—The following two commands will turn off CDP globally or on a specific interface:

```
no cdp run
no cdp enable
```

4.1.6—The following commands allow you to view, troubleshoot, and monitor CDP activity on your Cisco device:

```
clear cdp table
show debugging
debug cdp adjacency
debug cdp events
debug cdp ip
debug cdp packets
cdp timer
cdp holdtime
```

CCNA 2, Module 5

5.2.3 and 5.2.4—On Day 12, "Customize a Switch Configuration to Meet Specified Requirements and Manage System Image and Device Configuration Files (Two Objectives)," you reviewed the backup of configuration files using a TFTP server discussed in Module 3 from CCNA 2. Module 5 from CCNA 2 repeats this information and provides more detail on the use of HyperTerminal to capture a configuration. In HyperTerminal, you can use the menu items **Transfer > Capture Text** and then **Transfer > Send Text** to capture and then later place a configuration on a router.

CCNA 2, Module 9

9.3.3—As mentioned in Module 4 of CCNA 2, the **show cdp neighbors detail** command is a very valuable tool. This command displays device details such as the following items:

- Active interfaces
- Port ID
- Device type
- Cisco IOS version
- IP address of a neighboring device's interface

You have to bring the interface up with the **no shutdown** command and set a clock rate (if necessary) in order to receive CDP advertisements.

CCNA 3, Module 8

8.3.1 and 8.3.2—VLANs have become common in networks due to their ability to logically divide and organize traffic flow. You can use the following steps to troubleshoot VLANs:

Step 1   Check LEDs and cables.

Step 2   Pick one switch as a starting point and work outward.

Step 3   Check Layer 1.

Step 4   Check Layer 2.

Step 5   Check VLANs that span multiple switches.

Step 6   Look at traffic patterns and identify possible bottlenecks.

8.3.3–8.3.5—If Spanning Tree Protocol (STP) is not functioning properly, your network could be experiencing broadcast storms. If STP is running properly, you can then check other parameters with the following **show** commands, which allow you to look for errors in VLAN setup, protocols, and naming:

```
show vlan
show spanning-tree
debug sw-vlan packets
```

If you are having trouble establishing a trunk connection between a router and a switch, you can check the router interfaces and the Cisco IOS software trunking compatibility with the following commands:

```
show interfaces interface trunk
show interfaces interface switchport
show interface status
show running-config
show version
```

Summary

If you use the OSI model as a reference and the **cdp**, **debug**, and **show** commands outlined today, you have a great toolkit to solve LAN and VLAN issues. Pages 240–258 and 383–386 in the *CCNA Flash Cards and Exam Practice Pack* (CCNA Self-Study, exam #640-801), Second Edition, might also be helpful as you prepare for the CCNA exam.

Your Notes

Troubleshoot Routing Protocols

An advantage to using the command-line interface (CLI) of Cisco IOS software is your ability to use **show** and **debug** commands to obtain information about your network. The **show** commands can provide a valuable snapshot, whereas **debug** commands can display real-time routing protocol activity. The Cisco Networking Academy Program curriculum covers routing protocol–related troubleshooting commands in Modules 7 and 9 from CCNA 2 and in Modules 1, 2, and 3 from CCNA 3.

CCNA 2, Module 7

7.3.7 and 7.3.8—The following commands allow you to verify and troubleshoot routing protocols, including the Interior Gateway Routing Protocol (IGRP), as a specific example:

```
show interface
show running-config
show ip protocols
show ip route
debug ip igrp events
debug ip igrp transactions
ping
traceroute
```

CCNA 2, Module 9

9.1.1–9.1.9—Table 6-1 provides a definition and examples of troubleshooting and configuration commands that pertain to the routing table.

Table 6-1   **Routing Table–Related Troubleshooting**

Command	Examples	Definition
show ip route	show ip route rip	Displays routing table information.
	show ip route igrp	
	show ip route static	
	show ip route 192.168.5.0	
ip default-network	ip default-network 192.168.1.0	Sets a default route. The second example also defines a default route with a static route.
ip route 0.0.0.0/0	ip route 0.0.0.0 0.0.0.0 192.168.1.0	
show ip rip database	show ip rip database	Displays RIP updates.
show ip protocols	show ip protocols	Displays routing protocol information.

A quick look at the routing table can help you to determine which route has the lowest administrative distance. Default administrative distances for common routing protocols are listed in Table 6-2.

Table 6-2   Default Administrative Distances

Routing Protocol	Default Administrative Distance
Directly connected	0
Static	1 for a next hop IP address, 0 for an outgoing interface
EIGRP summary route	5
eBGP	20
EIGRP (internal)	90
IGRP	100
OSPF	110
IS-IS	115
RIP	120
EIGRP (external)	170
iBGP	200

CCNA 3, Module 1

1.2.5 and 1.2.6—The following commands allow you to verify and troubleshoot the Routing Information Protocol (RIP). Notice that the pattern of troubleshooting commands is similar for each protocol.

```
show ip protocols
show ip route
show ip interface brief
show running-config
debug ip rip
```

It is also useful to know that the **undebug all** or **no debug all** commands turn off all debugging.

CCNA 3, Module 2

2.3.7—If you have configured Open Shortest Path First (OSPF) and the routers are not communicating, you should consider the following possibilities:

- Make sure that the neighbors are sending hellos.

- Make sure that you do not have different hello and dead interval timers.

- Make sure that your interfaces are not on different network types.

- Make sure that authentication is set up correctly.

- Make sure that the addressing is set up correctly, including wildcard masks.

- Make sure that you have issued the **no shutdown** command for each interface.

CCNA 3, Module 3

3.3.1—When you are troubleshooting routing issues, consider the following points:

- Clearly define the problem and gather all the related facts.

- Create and implement an action plan.

- If the plan does not work, change one thing at a time until you can isolate the problem.

- Document the fix.

Table 6-3 provides the common troubleshooting commands for RIP, IGRP, EIGRP, and OSPF. Expect some repetition in commands.

Table 6-3   Troubleshooting Commands for Routing Protocols

Routing Protocol	Troubleshooting Commands
RIP	show running-config
	show ip protocols
	show ip route
	debug ip rip
IGRP	show running-config
	show ip protocols
	show ip route
	debug ip igrp
	debug ip igrp events
EIGRP	show running-config
	show ip protocols
	show ip eigrp neighbors
OSPF	show running-config
	show ip protocols
	show ip route
	show ip ospf neighbor
	debug ip ospf events
	debug ip ospf packet

Summary

The absolute best way to learn these commands is to have someone else royally mess up your network routing configurations and put you to work finding the errors. You can also pick out the troubleshooting command questions from pages 425–454 of the *CCNA Flash Cards and Exam Practice Pack* (CCNA Self-Study, exam #640-801), Second Edition for a quick review.

Your Notes

Troubleshoot IP Addressing and Host Configuration

When you understand the design and configuration of a network, simple commands such as **ping** and **telnet** provide great troubleshooting tools. The extended **ping** command on a router enables you to set very specific options when testing your IP configurations. The Cisco Networking Academy Program discusses IP addressing troubleshooting commands in Modules 4 and 9 of CCNA 2.

CCNA 2, Module 4

4.2.1–4.2.6—A quick way to test all seven layers of the OSI model is with the **telnet** command. Telnet operates at the application layer of the OSI model and allows you to connect remotely to another router. All configurations and protocols have to function correctly to support a Telnet session. You can specify up to five (0 through 4) vty sessions on a router to allow incoming Telnet connections to your router. If you telnet to a router by hostname, you need to make sure that you have configured Domain Name System (DNS) or the **ip host** command on your router. The following command will initiate a Telnet session with another router:

```
telnet {remote-router-ip-address ¦ remote-router-hostname}
```

Example 5-1   Initiate a Telnet Session Using an IP Address

```
Router#telnet 192.168.0.2
```

Example 5-2   Initiate a Telnet Session Using a Hostname

```
Router#telnet RouterB
```

You can suspend a Telnet session with the **Ctrl-Shift-6,** then **x** key combination. To view all of your sessions, you can type **show sessions**; and to disconnect a specific session, you can type **disconnect** followed by the host or IP address. You can resume a session by using the **resume** command followed by the host or IP address or by using the **Enter** key.

If Telnet does not function, you can test Layer 3 network connectivity using the following commands:

```
ping
traceroute
show ip route
```

CCNA 2, Module 9

9.2.5—To use the extended **ping** command, you type **ping** and press **Enter** and then specify the options shown in Example 5-3.

Example 5-3   The Extended ping Command

```
Router#ping
Protocol [ip]:
Target IP address:192.168.0.2
Repeat count [5]:
Datagram size [100]:
Timeout in seconds [2]:
Extended commands [n]:y
Source address or interface:192.168.0.1
Type of service [0]:
Set DF bit in IP header? [no]:
Validate reply data? [no]:
Data pattern [0xABCD]:
Loose, Strict, Record, Timestamp, Verbose[none]:
Sweep range of sizes [n]:
```

Summary

Often a mistyped IP address or incorrectly configured subnet mask proves to be the problem in a network that will not return a successful ping. This short chapter just begs you to take a CCNA practice exam today. Schedule a Cisco Networking Academy practice CCNA exam with your instructor or use the exam on the CD-ROM that accompanies the *CCNA Flash Cards and Exam Practice Pack* (CCNA Self-Study, exam #640-801), Second Edition. You could also flip through pages 255–258 in the *CCNA Flash Cards* book.

Your Notes

Troubleshoot a Device as Part of a Working Network

Today combines with Day 5, "Troubleshoot IP Addressing and Host Configuration," and Day 6, "Troubleshoot Routing Protocols," as a review of key **show**, **debug**, and connectivity-related commands. These troubleshooting topics originate from Module 1 from CCNA 1 and Modules 2, 4, 5, and 9 from CCNA 2.

CCNA 1, Module 1

1.1.9—You can use the same basic steps to troubleshoot all network devices:

Step 1   Collect information.

Step 2   Cycle through each layer of the OSI model to fix the problem starting at Layer 1.

Step 3   Document your work.

CCNA 2, Module 2

2.2.9 and 2.2.10—As you troubleshoot a router, some commands may not work. You can look for the carat symbol (^) to determine the portion of the command that the router did not understand. If part of the command was understood, you can type that portion of the command followed by a question mark (?) to view the options for that command. You can also use the **show version** command to determine the Cisco IOS software version running on the router and what commands are supported.

CCNA 2, Module 4

4.2.5 and 4.2.6—As mentioned on Day 5, the **ping** and **traceroute** commands allow you to check Layer 3 connectivity on your network. Once you have verified Layer 3 connectivity, you can use Telnet to test all seven layers of the OSI model.

CCNA 2, Module 5

5.2.4—As described on Day 12, "Customize a Switch Configuration to Meet Specified Requirements and Manage System Image and Device Configuration Files (Two Objectives)," and Day 7, "Perform LAN and VLAN Troubleshooting," you can quickly fix a configuration issue with a router by restoring an earlier running-config capture with your terminal program. Before restoring a captured configuration, be sure to delete unwanted text and add **no shutdown** to all configured interfaces.

CCNA 2, Module 9

9.3.4–9.3.7—Table 4-1 provides a list of some common troubleshooting commands and tactics:

Table 4-1   Troubleshooting Commands

Command	Definition
show ip route	Allows you to view all information provided to the router through configured routing protocols, including connected and known networks. If **show ip route** provides no information other than connected routes, you can check configured routing protocols with the **show ip protocols** command.
show ip protocols	Displays configured protocols, networks that are being advertised, the source of routing updates, and which interfaces are sending updates.
show controllers	If a cable is connected, displays the type of cable that is connected and whether clocking is detected on the interfaces of the router. If you are remotely connected to a router and cannot physically inspect the cables, this command is useful.
debug	Shows events on the router as they occur, including error messages, protocol events, and interface events. **Debug** can be processor intense and should be used only to troubleshoot. The **debug all** command displays all events and uses system resources to the point that it should not be implemented on a production router. The command **undebug all** or **no debug all** turns off all debugging.
terminal monitor	Redirects debug information to a remote terminal session.
traceroute	Identifies each hop on a path between two destinations. The **traceroute** command allows you to isolate the interface that is dropping packets on a network.

Summary

As mentioned yesterday, you need to spend time using these troubleshooting commands to identify and fix network issues. Lab time or practice with a simulator will strengthen your knowledge of these topics. Pages 231–238 of the *CCNA Flash Cards and Exam Practice Pack* (CCNA Self-Study, exam #640-801), Second Edition also review these topics.

Your Notes

Troubleshoot an Access List

The final installment in the review about access lists provides a list of **show** commands outlined in Module 11 from CCNA 2 that help you to see how the lists are configured. Keep in mind that troubleshooting also requires you to review your design and protocols to check access list functionality. Do not forget that all statements end with an implicit deny by default unless you specify otherwise.

CCNA 2, Module 11

11.1.5—You can test your access lists by creating sample traffic on your network, and you can verify access lists with the commands outlined in Table 3-1.

Table 3-1   **Access List show Commands**

Command	Function
show ip interface	Displays interface information, including whether an access list is assigned
show access-lists	Displays all access lists on a router
show running-config	Shows the entire running configuration, including access list configurations

11.2.4—Where you place an ACL on a router can affect how it filters packets. Remember that you place standard access lists as close to the destination of the traffic you want to filter and place extended access lists as close to the source of the traffic you want to filter. One way to remember this is to think that you always *stand at your destination* when you arrive. *Stand...stand*ard, ok...anyway.

Summary

Short day. Take, or retake, a Cisco Academy online practice CCNA exam and then have somebody wreak havoc on an access list configuration for you to fix. Pages 473–476 in the *CCNA Flash Cards and Exam Practice Pack* (CCNA Self-Study, exam #640-801), Second Edition can help you review today as well.

Your Notes

Perform Simple WAN Troubleshooting

Cisco IOS software provides a number of **show** and **debug** commands to troubleshoot WAN connectivity. These commands are outlined in Modules 3, 4, and 5 of CCNA 4 in the Cisco Networking Academy curriculum. As you recognize these commands, it is important to note the protocol and concept that you are troubleshooting.

CCNA 4, Module 3

3.3.5—To troubleshoot a serial connection, you can verify PPP encapsulation with the **show interface** command and use the **debug ppp** command. Table 2-1 displays all the options that you can use with the **debug ppp** command.

Table 2-1   PPP Troubleshooting

Command	Definition
debug ppp authentication	Displays authentication messages between routers
debug ppp packet	Displays sent and received PPP packets
debug ppp negotiation	Displays PPP packets during PPP startup as negotiation occurs
debug ppp error	Displays PPP protocol errors and statistics
debug ppp chap	Displays Challenge Handshake Authentication Protocol (CHAP) packets

CCNA 4, Module 4

4.2.4—You can verify ISDN with the following commands:

```
show interface
show isdn status
```

If **show isdn status** does not show Layer 1 as ACTIVE and Layer 2 as MULTIPLE_FRAME_ESTABLISHED, you can use the following two commands to view ISDN Layer 2 messages:

```
debug isdn q921
debug isdn q931
```

You can also use the **debug ppp** commands previously discussed to identify and troubleshoot Layer 2 issues.

4.3.9—The commands in Table 2-2 provide troubleshooting information for dial-on-demand routing (DDR).

Table 2-2   DDR Troubleshooting

Command	Definition
Debug isdn q921	Used to observe signaling events between the router and the ISDN switch, such as obtaining a terminal endpoint identifier (TEI) dynamically
Debug isdn q931	Displays call setup information for outgoing and incoming calls
Debug dialer packets	Displays DDR link connections and interesting traffic that caused the connection
Debug dialer events	Displays packets sent to the DDR interface
isdn call interface *interface*	Forces the local router to dial the remote router
Clear isdn bri	Clears established connections and resets the interface

CCNA 4, Module 5

5.2.6—The following commands can be used to verify Frame Relay:

```
show interfaces
show frame-relay lmi
show frame-relay pvc
show frame-relay map
```

5.2.7—The command **debug frame-relay lmi** allows you to view sent and received Local Management Interface (LMI) packets. A type 0 full LMI status message can provide further information with the following hex values:

- The value 0x0 indicates added/inactive or that the data-link connection identifier (DLCI) is programmed but not usable.

- The value 0x2 indicates added/active or that the DLCI is usable and functioning properly.

- The value 0x4 indicates deleted or that the DLCI was programmed at one point, but is no longer programmed.

Summary

Test the commands described today on a router if you have time. The more you see the output and recognize key variables, the quicker you will be able to answer related questions in the CCNA exam. Pages 541–546 and 571–574 in the *CCNA Flash Cards and Exam Practice Pack* (CCNA Self-Study, exam #640-801), Second Edition also review WAN troubleshooting and verification.

Your Notes

Key Points from Each Day for Relaxed Skimming

Today you should try to take a timed practice test using either the Cisco Academy practice CCNA or the exam simulation that accompanies the *CCNA Flash Cards and Exam Practice Pack* (CCNA Self-Study, exam #640-801), Second Edition. Today you also focus on the common CCNA details that may show up on the exam. Something as simple as a default TCP port number or a default administrative distance can quickly highlight the correct answer in the CCNA exam. The following sections outline the details from each day that you should feel comfortable with, or at least be able to recognize as part of a larger concept. Treat today as if you were skimming through a configuration file to find the key details of a router configuration.

Day 31

The benefits of using a layered model are as follows:

- Reduces complexity

- Standardizes interfaces

- Facilitates modular engineering

- Ensures interoperable technology

- Accelerates evolution

- Simplifies teaching and learning

Table 1-1 provides an overview of both the TCP/IP model and the OSI model, including a short description and the protocol data unit (PDU) for each layer.

Table 1-1   The TCP/IP Model Versus the OSI Model

TCP/IP Model	OSI Model	Key Points	PDU
4 Application	7 Application	User interaction	Data
	6 Presentation	Encryption and compression	Data
	5 Session	Session control, SQL	Data
3 Transport	4 Transport	End-to-end communications, TCP and UDP	Segments
2 Internet	3 Network	Path determination, routers	Packets
1 Network Access	2 Data link	LLC and MAC, switch	Frames
	1 Physical	Media and signals, hub	Bits

Table 1-2   Application Layer Protocols and Transport Layer Ports

Application Layer Protocol	Transport Layer Port/Protocol
http	Port 80 TCP Connection-Oriented
FTP	Port 21 TCP Connection-Oriented
FTP-Data	Port 20 TCP Connection-Oriented
Telnet	Port 23 TCP Connection-Oriented
SMTP	Port 25 TCP Connection-Oriented
DNS	Port 53 UDP and TCP
TFTP	Port 69 UDP Connectionless
SNMP	Port 161 UDP Connectionless

Day 30

Switches perform the following Spanning Tree Protocol (STP) actions to prevent loops in a redundant switched network:

- **Send out bridge protocol data units (BPDUs)**—Each switch sends BPDUs that include the bridge ID (BID) containing the bridge priority and MAC address.

- **Elect a root bridge**—The switch with the lowest bridge priority becomes the root bridge.

- **Specify a root port**—The port with the best bandwidth connection (lowest cost path) becomes the root or designated port.

- **Cycle ports through the STP states**—After the network has converged, all ports are in the blocking or forwarding state until there is a topology change. Table 1-3 describes the port states.

Table 1-3   Spanning-Tree Port States

Port State	Description
Blocking	The port looks only at BPDUs.
Listening	The port checks for multiple paths to the root bridge and blocks all ports *except* the port with the lowest cost path to the root bridge.
Learning	The port learns MAC addresses but does not forward data.
Forwarding	The port learns MAC addresses, forwards data, and processes BPDUs.

Day 29

Table 1-4 describes the different LAN topologies. These topologies can describe logical or physical characteristics of a LAN.

Table 1-4   LAN Topologies

Topology	Description
Bus	All devices are connected. Ethernet is a logical bus topology. Uses CSMA/CD.
Ring	Hosts connected to other hosts. FDDI is a logical ring topology. This topology is deterministic.
Star	All devices connected to a hub or switch. Ethernet is an example of a nondeterministic physical star topology.
Hierarchal	A pyramid of physical star networks connected to a main proxy.
Mesh	All devices connected to all other devices.

Switches can operate in cut-through or store-and-forward modes:

- **Store-and-forward**—Store-and-forward mode results in the switch receiving the *entire* frame before forwarding the information.

- **Cut-through**—In cut-through mode, a switch either sends the frame as soon as it knows the destination MAC address (*fast-forward*) or the switch reads the first 64 bytes and then sends the frame (*fragment-free*).

Day 28

Table 1-5 compares the features of distance vector and link-state protocols.

Table 1-5   Distance Vector and Link-State Protocols

Distance Vector	Link-State
Routers send periodic updates of the entire routing table to neighbors.	Routers send link-state advertisements (LSAs) to update other routers.
	Routers flood LSAs only when there is a topology change.
Routers see only neighboring routers.	Routers use the LSAs to build a full topology of the network.
Routers use a metric to determine the cost path for a route and build a routing table.	Routers use the Shortest Path First (SPF) algorithm and LSAs to build a shortest path tree as well as a routing table.
	To develop a full loop-free topological database requires more memory in a router.

Routers can avoid loops with the following tactics:

- You can combine route poisoning with the maximum hop count, triggered updates, and a holddown timer to prevent routing loops.

- Split horizon does not allow a router to send an update for a route to the router that originally advertised the route.

- If you were to run Open Shortest Path First (OSPF) on a fiber network, all routers would technically be connected on the fiber ring to each other. This means that each router would be a neighbor to every other router. OSPF avoids a network of never-ending neighbors with an election. Routers that are connected on broadcast multiaccess networks such as fiber or Ethernet or nonbroadcast multiaccess networks such as Frame Relay elect a single router called the designated router (DR) to handle updates. To avoid a single point of failure, they also elect a backup designated router (BDR).

- OSPF hello packets typical to link-state protocols go out over the multicast address 224.0.0.5. If the connection is point-to-point, the hellos go out every ten seconds. If the connection is multiaccess, the packets go out every 30 seconds.

- Enhanced Interior Gateway Routing Protocol (EIGRP) uses a neighboring table in the same way that OSPF uses an adjacency database to maintain information on adjacent routers. EIGRP, however, uses a distance-vector diffusing update algorithm (DUAL) to recalculate a topology.

- The neighboring and topology table allow EIGRP to use DUAL to identify the best route, or the *successor route*, and enter it into the routing table. Backup routes, or *feasible successor routes*, are kept only in the topology table.

- EIGRP sends hello packets on 224.0.0.10 to communicate with neighbors.

Day 27

Table 1-6 explains Class A, B, C, D, and E IP addresses.

Table 1-6   Class A, B, C, D, and E IP Addresses

Class	Binary Start	1st Octet Range	Network (N) and host (H) Octets	Number of Hosts	Bits in Network Address
Class A	0	1–126*	N.H.H.H	About 16 million	8
Class B	10	128–191	N.N.H.H	65,535	16
Class C	110	192–223	N.N.N.H	254	24
Class D	1110	224–239	H.H.H.H	Multicast	28
Class E	1111	240–255	RESEARCH	RESEARCH	RESEARCH

* The Class A address 127.0.0.0 is reserved for the loopback.

The following points discuss ARP, IP, and TCP functions:

- Address Resolution Protocol (ARP) finds a MAC address using the IP address. ARP occurs when a host has a destination IP address for a packet but needs to determine the MAC address to send the packet over the LAN.

- TCP uses positive acknowledgment, sliding windows, and a three-way handshake and is the Layer 4 connection-oriented protocol.

- User Datagram Protocol (UDP) is the Layer 4 connectionless protocol and relies on upper layers for error correction.

- The process in sliding windows where TCP requests that a host resend information is called *positive acknowledgement and retransmission (PAR)*.

- A more concise definition of port number ranges includes well-known ports (0 to 1023), registered ports (1024 to 49151), and dynamic ports (49152 to 65535).

- A host can provide services simultaneously on two different ports. An example could be a web server that provides HTTP access on port 80 at the same time as Telnet access on port 23.

- Port number assignment occurs at Layer 4 of the OSI model, IP address assignment occurs at Layer 3, and MAC address assignment occurs at Layer 2.

Day 26

Consider the following full image name:

C2600-is-mz

The following defines the image name sections:

- C2600 = platform = Cisco 2600 series
- is = feature set = IP Plus
- mz = image location/compression = RAM/zipped

When a Cisco router powers up, it first performs a power-on self test (POST), loads a bootstrap, and initializes the IOS from flash, a TFTP server, or ROM. The location of the IOS can be specified in the configuration register. Once the IOS is loaded, it loads the configuration file from NVRAM. If there is no configuration file in NVRAM, the Cisco IOS software searches for a TFTP server to load the configuration file. If there is no TFTP server, the IOS starts the setup dialog.

Day 25

A *local collision* occurs when a network card notices that the receive (RX) wires and the send (TX) wires are active at the same time.

A *remote collision* occurs when a frame is too small but does show the same symptoms as a local collision. A remote collision is likely the result of a local collision on the other side of a hub or repeater. The repeater would only regenerate the bad frame and not the simultaneous TX and RX.

A *late collision* occurs after the first 64 bits of data have been transmitted for a frame. The Layer 2 network card cannot recognize this type of collision and must rely on the upper layers to request retransmission.

A *runt* is a frame that is below the minimum size of 64 octets. Runts are usually made up of collision fragments. A frame that exceeds the maximum legal frame size will cause a network diagnostic tool to report jabber on the connection. If a frame does not match its own frame check sequence (FCS), it is considered a cyclic redundancy check (CRC) error.

A binary 1 means ignore and a binary 0 means match in a wildcard mask. Do not look for a relationship between wildcard masks and subnet masks; wildcard masks serve an entirely different function from subnet masks. The wildcard mask 0.0.0.0 states that the access control list (ACL) should match the entire host. 0.0.0.0 can also be represented by the term **any** or **host** in an ACL.

Day 24

A WAN connection uses a Layer 2 frame to encapsulate data.

Some common data link layer WAN encapsulation types include the following:

- Cisco proprietary HDLC
- PPP
- LAPB

Frame Relay is an example of a Layer 2 WAN connection-oriented packet-switching system where the route is determined by switches and each frame carries an identifier called a data-link connection identifier (DLCI).

Frame Relay switches create a virtual circuit (VC) between communicating hosts that exists only when the frame is being transferred. The VC is identified by the DLCI.

ISDN bearer (B) channels carry data at 64 kbps for each channel. The ISDN delta (D) channel is used to set up the call and for signaling. The call with Integrated Services Digital Network (ISDN) is faster than a modem, and the ISDN connection allows for a PPP-encapsulated link.

Dial-on-demand routing (DDR) interesting traffic is network activity that causes a router to connect to a network. You can define a dialer-list on a Cisco router that tells the router what traffic should cause it to bring up a DDR link.

Day 23

RFC 1918 states that there are reserved Class A, B, and C address ranges for private LANs. The private ranges are as follows:

- Class A 10.0.0.0 to 10.255.255.255
- Class B 172.16.0.0 to 172.31.255.255
- Class C 192.168.0.0 to 192.168.255.255

Table 1-7 outlines LAN design considerations divided by OSI layer.

Table 1-7   **LAN Design by OSI Layer**

OSI Layer	Design Considerations
Network (3)	Routers commonly forward data based on IP addressing and connect LANs and divide broadcast domains between LANs. Routers can also act as firewalls and provide a WAN connection. You can divide Layer 2 switches into VLANs to separate networks at Layer 3, but you need a router to communicate between VLANs.
Data link (2)	To microsegment collision domains you should use switches. Switch ports have only two hosts per collision domain with a source and destination host. The use of hubs instead of switches increases the size of collision domains to all hosts connected and affects bandwidth.
Physical (1)	Fiber optic for distances over 100 meters and unshielded twisted pair (UTP) for 100 meters or less. The main distribution facility (MDF) connects through the vertical cross-connects (VCCs) to the intermediate distribution facilities (IDFs), which connect through horizontal cross-connects (HCCs) to hosts.

Day 22

You can use Table 1-8 to quickly determine the details necessary to subnet a Class C network.

Table 1-8   Class C Subnet Chart

Bits Borrowed	1	2	3	4	5	6	7	8
Slash format	/25	/26	/27	/28	/29	/30	/31	/32
Mask	128	192	224	240	248	252	254	255
Bits borrowed	1	2	3	4	5	6	7	8
Total subnets	2*	4	8	16	32	64	N/A	N/A
Usable subnets*	0*	2*	6*	14*	30*	62*	N/A	N/A
Total hosts	128*	64	32	16	8	4	N/A	N/A
Usable hosts	126*	62	30	14	6	2	N/A	N/A

*Stars refer to CCNA 3, Module 1. The /25 subnet is sometimes usable as well as total subnets (all 0s and all 1s) in later versions of the IOS and if you enter the **ip subnet zero** command.

Day 21

Table 1-9 charts the routing protocols discussed in the Cisco Networking Academy curriculum.

Table 1-9   Routing Protocols

Protocol Name	AD	Type	Description
Routing Information Protocol (RIP)	120	Interior, distance vector	Broadcasts updates every 30 seconds and uses hop count as the metric with a maximum of 16.
Routing Information Protocol Version 2 (RIPv2)	120	Interior, distance vector	Multicasts updates every 30 seconds using the address 224.0.0.9 and includes subnet mask in updates.
OSPF	110	Interior, link-state	Nonproprietary protocol; updates only when there is a change in topology. Supports variable-length subnet mask (VLSM).
Interior Gateway Routing Protocol (IGRP)	100	Interior, distance vector	Broadcasts updates every 90 seconds and uses bandwidth, load, and delay as a metric.
EIGRP	90	Interior, hybrid	Uses both link-state and distance vector features and multicasts updates on 224.0.0.10. Supports VLSM.
Border Gateway Protocol (BGP)	20	Exterior, distance vector	Used to route between autonomous systems.

Day 20

Table 1-10 defines four types of internetworks.

Table 1-10   Network Types

Network Type	Designed To:
Wide-area network (WAN)	Connect LANs using serial interfaces over a large geographic area to provide remote resources, e-mail, and Internet access.
Metropolitan-area network (MAN)	Connect LANs in a metropolitan area using private lines, a wireless bridge, or optical services.
Storage-area network (SAN)	Provide high-performance, fault-tolerant, scalable storage for servers over a separate network from the client/server network.
Virtual private network (VPN)	Provide a private network that exists inside of a public network. Clients connect through a secure tunnel to the VPN router at the destination.

Day 19

Remember the following points about ACLs:

- The way to revise an ACL is to delete and recreate it unless you are using a named ACL and can add statements to the end.

- A router checks ACL statements in the order in which you create them.

- A router stops checking ACL statements after the first match.

- At the end of every ACL, there is an implicit deny.

- You can apply to each interface one ACL per protocol per direction.

- Place extended ACLs closest to the source.

- Place standard ACLs closest to the destination.

- An ACL should filter specific addresses first and then groups of addresses.

- Do not work with an access list that is applied and active.

- When an IP ACL rejects a packet, it sends an ICMP implicit deny.

- Outbound ACLs do not affect traffic originating from the router.

Day 18

WAN protocols operate at the physical and data link layers of the OSI seven-layer reference model. Table 1-11 highlights key points about ISDN, Frame Relay, and ATM, and Table 1-12 describes PPP session establishment.

Table 1-11   WAN Connection and Protocol Examples

WAN Protocol	Network Type	Key Points
ISDN	Circuit-switched	BRI has 1 channel for signaling and 2 channels for data. PRI has 1 signaling channel and 23 data channels.
Frame Relay	Packet-switched	Uses DLCIs to identify circuits and LMI messages to learn about the network.
ATM	Cell-switched	High-bandwidth WAN protocol that uses a 53-byte cell. Good for video and streaming applications.

Table 1-12   PPP Session Establishment

Phase	Description
Link-establishment phase	Each device sends Link Control Protocol (LCP) frames and negotiates LCP options; then LCP opens the connection with a configuration acknowledgment frame.

continues

Table 1-12   PPP Session Establishment   *continued*

Phase	Description
Authentication phase (optional)	The established link can authenticate using Password Authentication Protocol (PAP) or Challenge Handshake Authentication Protocol (CHAP) and also check link quality.
Network layer protocol phase	PPP devices send Network Control Protocol (NCP) packets to configure network layer protocols and allow Layer 3 transmission.

The three categories of ISDN protocols are as follows:

- **E series**—Telephone network standards

- **I series**—ISDN concepts and terminology

- **Q series**—How switching and call setup (signaling) function, including Q.921 link access procedure on the D channel (LAPD) and the Q.931 ISDN network layer

The following two examples describe ISDN reference points:

- You have a TE1 that is a native ISDN interface that connects at the S reference to the customer switching network termination type 2 (NT2). The NT2 connects at the T reference to the network termination type 1 (NT1), and the NT1 connects at the U reference to the local loop.

- You have a TE2 that is not native ISDN, so you first connect at the R reference to the terminal adapter (TA) and then to the NT2. The NT2 connects at the T reference to the NT1, and the NT1 connects at the U reference to the local loop.

S and T references can be similar, so you may sometimes see an S/T interface.

Day 17

Table 1-13 lists the syntax for different types of routing protocols.

Table 1-13   Routing Protocol Command Syntax

Protocol	Commands
Static	**ip route** *destination-network subnet-mask* {*outgoing-interface*	*next-hop-address*}
Default	**ip route** 0.0.0.0 0.0.0.0 {*outgoing-interface*	*next-hop-address*}
RIP	**router rip**
	network *directly-connected-network*
IGRP	**router igrp** *autonomous-system-number*
	network *directly-connected-network*
OSPF	**router ospf** *process-id*
	network *network-address wildcard-mask* **area** *area-id*
	exit

Protocol	Commands
	interface loopback 0
	ip address *ip-address subnet-mask*
OSPF simple authentication	**interface** *interface*
	ip ospf authentication-key *password*
	exit
	area *area-number* **authentication**
OSPF authentication with MD5	**interface** *interface*
	ip ospf message-digest-key *key-id* **md5** *key*
	area *area-number* **authentication message-digest**
	exit
	router ospf *process id*
	area *area-id* **authentication message-digest**
EIGRP	**router eigrp** *autonomous-system-number*
	network *network-number*
	eigrp log-neighbor-changes
	bandwidth *bandwidth*
	no auto-summary

Day 16

You use the following command syntax to configure a serial interface. You will only use the **clock rate** command if the interface is data communications equipment (DCE).

```
interface type slot/port
ip address ip-address netmask
clock rate clock-rate
no shutdown
```

Example 1-1   Configuring a Serial Interface

```
Router>enable
Router#configure terminal
Router(config)#interface serial 0/0
Router(config-if)#ip address 172.16.1.1 255.255.255.0
Router(config-if)#clock rate 56000
Router(config-if)#no shutdown
```

Day 15

Table 1-14 and Table 1-15 recount additional router configurations such as console, vty, NAT, and DHCP.

Table 1-14   Set the Console and vty Passwords

Console Password Configuration	VTY Password Configuration
line console 0	line vty 0 4
password cisco	password cisco
login	login

Table 1-15   NAT and DHCP Configuration Commands

Static NAT Configuration	DHCP Configuration
ip nat inside source static *local-IP global-IP*	ip dhcp pool *pool-name*
interface *interface*	network *network-address subnet-mask*
ip nat outside	default-router *default-router-address*
interface *interface*	dns-server *dns-server-address*
ip nat inside	domain-name *domain-name*

Example 1-2   NAT Configuration with Overload for One Outside IP Address

```
Router(config)#access-list 1 permit 192.168.1.0 0.0.0.255
Router(config)#ip nat inside source list 1 interface serial 0 overload
Router(config)#interface serial 0
Router(config-if)#ip nat outside
Router(config-if)#interface fa 0/0
Router(config-if)#ip nat inside
```

Example 1-3   NAT Configuration with Overload for a Pool of Outside IP Addresses

```
Router(config)#access-list 1 permit 192.168.1.0 0.0.0.255
Router(config)#ip nat pool isp-pool 209.165.200.225 209.165.200.235 netmask
255.255.255.224
Router(config)#ip nat inside source list 1 pool isp-pool overload
Router(config)#interface serial 0
Router(config-if)#ip nat outside
Router(config-if)#interface fa 0/0
Router(config-if)#ip nat inside
```

Day 14

Remember the following points about VLANs:

- VLAN membership is based on job assignment regardless of location (referred to as end-to-end). However, due to the wide use of Internet access, geographic VLANs have become more common than end-to-end VLANs.

- VLAN membership can be configured to follow the users when they change location on the network in an end-to-end network, but as previously stated geographic VLANs are more common.

- VLAN membership provides security settings assigned for each logical group.

- The two types of frame tagging are Cisco proprietary Inter-Switch Link (ISL) and IEEE 802.1Q. You would use 802.1q to connect a Cisco switch to a non-Cisco device.

Table 1-16 and Table 1-17 define Virtual Terminal Protocol (VTP) modes and provide static VLAN, trunk, and VTP configuration commands.

Table 1-16   VTP Switch Modes

VTP Mode	Capabilities	Definition
Server	Can create, modify, and delete VLANs	Sends VTP messages out all trunk ports and saves VLAN configuration in the NVRAM.
Client	Cannot create, modify, and delete VLANs	Better for switches that do not have enough memory for large configurations. VTP clients process changes and forward messages.
Transparent	Only forward advertisements	Does not modify its VLAN database, but forwards received VTP messages.

Table 1-17   Switch Static VLAN, Trunk, and VTP Configuration Commands

Configuration Type	Commands
Static VLAN	**vlan database**
	vlan *vlan-number*
	interface *interface*
	switchport access vlan *vlan-number*
Trunk	**switchport trunk encapsulation** {*isl* | *dot1q*}
VTP	**vlan database**
	vtp v2-mode
	vtp domain *domain*
	vtp {*client* | *server* | *transparent*}
	vtp password *password*

Day 13

Table 1-18 provides a description for different types of UTP networking cable.

Table 1-18   UTP Cabling for Network Devices

Cable	Used to Connect	Description
Crossover cable	Switch to switch	TIA/EIA-568-A on one end and TIA/EIA-568-B on the other end.
	Switch to hub	
	Hub to hub	
	Router to router	
	Host/server to host	
	Router to host	
Straight-through cable	Router to switch	TIA/EIA-568-A on both ends or TIA/EIA-568-B on both ends.
	Router to hub	
	Host/server to switch	
	Host/server to hub	
Rollover cable	Terminal to console port on a device for configuration, typically a serial port on a host to a console port on a router or switch	Pins 1–8 reversed on either end. Often converted to 9-pin serial on one end.

Day 12

Bridges and switches divide collision domains and filter at Layer 2. Each port on a bridge or switch is microsegmented into its own collision domain. Layer 2 switches can also divide broadcast domains with VLANs, but you need a router to communicate between VLANs.

Layer 3 switches and routers filter at Layer 3 of the OSI model and divide broadcast domains.

A router starts using the following sequence:

1. The router checks the hardware (POST) and loads the bootstrap code from the read-only memory (ROM).

2. The router first looks for the Cisco IOS software in the flash memory, then looks for a TFTP server that could have the IOS, and lastly, if there is no other option, loads a stripped version of the IOS from ROM.

3. Once the Cisco IOS software is loaded, the router first looks for a configuration file in the NVRAM, then looks for a TFTP server that might have the configuration, and lastly, if there

is no configuration, outputs a set of questions to the console to ask the user for configuration parameters.

Table 1-19 lists router configuration and backup commands.

Table 1-19   Router Configuration and Image Backup Commands

Configuration Backup	Image Backup
copy running-config tftp	copy flash tftp
copy tftp running-config	copy tftp flash
	xmodem -c *image-file-name*
	set
	tftpdnld
	Cisco IOS release 12.0 and later:
	copy *location:URL location:URL*

The following commands allow you to define how a router will boot:

```
boot system flash IOS-filename
boot system tftp IOS-filename tftp-address
boot system rom
config-register configuration-register-value
```

Table 1-20 deciphers the values in the configuration register.

Table 1-20   Configuration Register Values

Register Value	Example	Description
0x___0	0x2100	System enters ROM monitor mode. Use **b** to boot the system.
0x___1	0x2101	Boots the first image in flash. This setting will boot the limited ROM version on older platforms.
0x___2 to 0x___F	0x2142, 0x2102	Looks in the NVRAM for boot system commands. The specific example 0x2142 ignores any configuration in the NVRAM. If there are no commands, the system boots the first image in flash. 0x2102 would apply the configuration in the NVRAM.

If your router boots to a nonconfigured router (and you saved to startup-config), use the **show version** command to see if the configuration register value is 0x2142.

Day 11

Table 1-21 and Table 1-22 cover the keystrokes used in the Cisco IOS software as well as editing commands and initial router commands.

Table 1-21   Cisco IOS Editing Keys and Commands

Command/Keystroke	Definition
Tab	Automatically complete a command
Ctrl-P or Up Arrow	Repeat previously typed commands
Ctrl-A	Move to the beginning of a command line
Esc-B	Move back one word
Ctrl-B or Left Arrow	Move back one character
Ctrl-E	Move to the end of the command line
Ctrl-F or Right Arrow	Move forward one character
Esc-F	Move forward one word
Ctrl-Z	Exit configuration mode
show history	Display the command buffer
terminal history size *number*	Set the history buffer size
terminal no editing	Turn off advanced editing
terminal editing	Enable advanced editing

Table 1-22   Common Initial Router Commands and Switch Commands

Router Commands	Switch Commands
enable	**enable**
configure terminal	**configure terminal**
hostname *hostname*	**hostname** *hostname*
banner motd	**copy running-config startup-config**
enable secret *password*	
copy running-config startup-config	

Day 10

Table 1-23 provides the commands needed to configure different ACLs.

Table 1-23   Access List Commands

ACL Type	ACL Commands
Standard	**access-list** *ACL-number* {**deny** I **permit**} *source-address wildcard*
	ip access-group *ACL-number* {**in** I **out**}
Extended	**access-list** *ACL-number* {**deny** I **permit**} *protocol source wildcard-mask destination wildcard-mask operator port*
	ip access-group *ACL-number* {**in** I **out**}
Restrict VTY	**access-list** *ACL-number* {**deny** I **permit**} *source-address wildcard-mask*
	ip access-class *ACL-number* {**in** I **out**}
Named ACL	**access-list** {**extended** I **standard**} *name*
	{**deny** I **permit**} *protocol source wildcard destination wildcard-mask operator port*
	ip access-group *ACL-number* {**in** I **out**}

You can use numbers from the following ranges to identify a numbered access list:

- **Standard IP ACL**—Numbers 1–99 or 1300–1999
- **Extended IP**—Numbers 100–199 or 2000–2699
- **AppleTalk**—Numbers 600–699

Day 9

Table 1-24 lists the commands that you would use for PPP, ISDN, DDR, and Frame Relay.

Table 1-24   WAN Configuration Commands

Protocol	Basic Commands
PPP	**encapsulation ppp**
	compress {**predictor** I **stac**}
	ppp quality {*1 to 100 as a percentage*}
	ppp multilink
	username *name* **password** *secret-password*
	encapsulation ppp
	ppp authentication {**chap** I **chap pap** I **pap chap** I **pap**}
	ppp pap sent-username *username* **password** *password*

continues

Table 1-24   WAN Configuration Commands   *continued*

Protocol	Basic Commands
ISDN BRI	**isdn switch-type** *switch-type*
	isdn spid{*number*} *spid-number local-dial-number*
	encapsulation ppp
ISDN PRI	**controller t1**
	framing {**sf** I **esf**}
	linecode {**ami** I **b8zs** I **hdb3**}
	pri-group timeslots *range*
	interface serial {*slot/port:* I *unit:*} {**23** I **15**}
	isdn switch-type *switch-type*
	controller e1
	framing {**crc4** I **no-crc4**}
	linecode {**ami** I **b8zs** I **hdb3**}
	pri-group timeslots *range*
	interface serial {*slot/port:* I *unit:*} {**23** I **15**}
	isdn switch-type *switch-type*
DDR, legacy	**dialer-list** *number* **protocol** *protocol* {**permit** I **deny** I **list** [*access-list-number*]}
	interface *interface*
	dialer-group *number*
	dialer idle-timeout *seconds-after-last-traffic*
	dialer map ip *next-hop* **name** *next-hop-hostname dial-number*
DDR, dialer profiles	**dialer-list** *number* **protocol** *protocol* {**permit** I **deny** I **list** [*access-list-number*]}
	interface dialer *virtual-interface-number*
	dialer-group *number*
	dialer remote name *next-hop-hostname*
	dialer string *dial-number*
	dialer-pool *number*
	dialer idle-timeout *seconds-after-last-traffic*
	dialer pool-member *number* **priority** *priority*
Frame Relay (no LMI)	**encapsulation frame-relay** {**cisco** I **ietf**}
	frame-relay map *protocol protocol-address dlci broadcast*
Frame Relay	**encapsulation frame-relay** {**cisco** I **ietf**}
	frame-relay lmi-type {**ansi** I **cisco** I **q933a**}
	interface serial *subinterface-number* {**point-to-point** I **multipoint**}
	frame-relay interface-dlci *DLCI-number*

Day 8

Table 1-25 pinpoints the common issues you encounter on a network in relation to the OSI seven-layer model.

Table 1-25   OSI Model Troubleshooting

Layer	Common Issues
Layers 7–4	Ping works, but Telnet does not work. Telnet tests all seven layers of the OSI model.
Layer 3	IP addressing and routing protocol configuration issues. Ping tests Layer 3.
Layer 2	Improper or missing configurations for clock rate and encapsulation.
Layer 1	Incorrect cables. DTE and DCE cable problems or transceiver issues. LED indicators and power LED–related issues.

Day 7

Make sure that you are familiar with the following commands for LAN and VLAN troubleshooting:

cdp run	**show debugging**
no cdp run	**debug cdp adjacency**
no cdp enable	**debug cdp events**
clear cdp counters	**debug cdp ip**
cdp enable	**debug cdp packets**
show cdp traffic	**cdp timer**
show cdp	**cdp holdtime**
show cdp neighbors	**show debug**
show cdp neighbors detail	**show vlan**
clear cdp table	

The command **show cdp** does not show information about neighboring devices. It tells you about the configuration of CDP on the device you are using. To see information about neighboring devices, use the command **show cdp neighbors**.

Day 6

Table 1-26 specifies the commands that can aid you while troubleshooting a routing protocol.

Table 1-26   Routing Protocol Troubleshooting

Commands	Default Administrative Distances
debug ip igrp events	Directly connected, 0
debug ip igrp transactions	Static, 1
ip default-network	EIGRP summary route, 5
ip route 0.0.0.0/0	eBGP, 20
show ip rip database	EIGRP (internal), 90
show ip interface brief	IGRP, 100
show running-config	OSPF, 110
undebug all	IS-IS, 115
no debug all	RIP, 120
show ip eigrp neighbors	EIGRP (external), 170
show ip ospf neighbor	iBGP, 200
debug ip ospf events	
debug ip ospf packet	

Days 5 and 4

Be sure to remember the commands, concepts, and key combinations that you can use with the Cisco IOS software while troubleshooting a network.

show ip route

show ip protocols

show controllers

debug all

terminal monitor

traceroute

ping

You can look for the carat symbol (^) to determine the portion of the command that the router did not understand. If part of the command was understood, you can type that portion of the command followed by a question mark (?) to view the options for that command. The **telnet** command can be suspended with the keystroke Ctrl-Shift-6, then x. You can look at all sessions with the command **show sessions** and use **disconnect** to disconnect a session and **resume** to resume a session.

Day 3

Tahe following **show** commands can help you troubleshoot an access list:

show access-lists

show ip interface

show running-config

Standard access lists should be placed as close to the destination of the traffic you want to filter, and extended access lists should be placed as close to the source of the traffic you want to filter.

Day 2

The following commands allow you to troubleshoot WAN protocols such as PPP, ISDN, and Frame Relay:

debug ppp authentication	**debug isdn q931**
debug ppp packet	**debug dialer packets**
debug ppp negotiation	**debug dialer events**
debug ppp error	**isdn call interface** *interface*
debug ppp chap	**clear isdn bri**
show isdn status	**debug frame-relay lmi**
debug isdn q921	

Remember that **debug** commands are an ongoing presentation of changes on a network, while **show** commands provide a specific snapshot for a point in time on a network. Use **debug** commands only when you are troubleshooting.

Summary

All the topics discussed today should be floating around in your head within reach for test day. What is possibly the most important factor for success on the exam is your attitude. Treat each detail like a familiar old friend and not a hard, cold obstacle. Read with a smile. Your passion for this subject will come through on test day just as clearly as it will come through in a job interview or planning meeting. I do realize that this last day is an abbreviation of my abbreviation of the Academy curriculum. All of the information in this book, the Cisco IOS software, and the Academy Curriculum can be whittled down to just one four-letter word on your resume: CCNA. Good luck on the test.

Your Notes

Part V

Exam Day and Post-Exam Information

Exam Day: Becoming a CCNA

Post-Exam: After the CCNA Exam

Becoming a CCNA

Today is your opportunity to prove that you know how to describe, plan, implement, and troubleshoot a network. Ninety minutes and 65 questions stand between you and your CCNA certification. Use the following information to focus on the details specific to the day of your CCNA exam.

What You Need for the Exam

Write the exam location, date, exam time, exam center phone number, and the proctor's name in the lines that follow:

Location: _____

Date: _____

Exam Time (arrive early): _____

Exam Center Phone Number: _____

Proctor's Name: _____

Remember the following items on Exam Day:

- You must have **two forms of ID** that include a photo and signature such as a driver's license, passport, or military identification.

- The test proctor will take you through the agreement and set up your testing station after you have signed the agreement.

- The test proctor will give you a sheet for scratch paper or a dry erase pad. Do not take these out of the room.

- The testing center will store any personal items while you take the exam. It is best to bring only what you will need.

- You will be monitored during the entire exam.

What You Should Receive After Completion

When you complete the exam, you will see an immediate electronic response as to whether you passed or failed. The proctor will give you a certified score report with the following important information:

- Your score based on a scale of 300 to 1000 points. The minimum score required to pass is around 800 (the minimum score listed on my last exam report was 849). The report will also include your percentage in the planning and design, implementation and operation, troubleshooting, and technology sections of the exam. Cisco.com explains that the scoring scale could change without notice, but the scoring has remained the same for the last three versions of the CCNA.

- Identification information that you will need to track your certification. *Do not lose your certified examination score report.*

Summary

Your state of mind is a key factor in your success on the CCNA exam. If you know the details of the curriculum and the details of the exam process, you can begin the exam with confidence and focus. Arrive early to the exam. Bring earplugs in the off chance that your testing neighbor has a bad cough or any loud nervous habits. Do not let an extremely difficult or specific question impede your progress. You cannot return to questions on the exam that you have already answered, so answer each question confidently and keep an eye on the timer.

After the CCNA

The accomplishment of signing up for and actually taking the CCNA exam is no small feat. Many network engineers have avoided the CCNA exam for years. The following sections discuss your options after test day.

Receiving Your Certificate

If you passed the exam, you will receive your official CCNA certificate and wallet card about six weeks (eight weeks internationally) after exam day. Your certificate will be mailed to the address you provided when you registered for the exam.

You will need your examination score report to log in to the certification tracking system and set up a login to check your certification status. If you do not receive your certificate, you have to open a case in the certificate online support located at the following web address:

http://ciscocert.custhelp.com/

When you receive your certificate, you may want to frame it and put it on a wall. A certificate hanging on a wall is much harder to lose than a certificate in a filing cabinet or random folder. You never know when an employer or academic institution could request a copy.

Your CCNA is valid for three years. To keep your certificate valid, you must pass the CCNA again or pass another Cisco exam in a path to a professional level certification before the end of the three year period.

Determining Career Options

After passing the CCNA exam, be sure to add your CCNA certification to your resume. Matthew Moran provides the following advice for adding certifications to a resume in his book, *The IT Career Builder's Toolkit* (Cisco Press, 2005. ISBN: 1587131560):

> *I don't believe you should place your certifications after your name. It is presumptuous to pretend that your latest certification is the equivalent to someone who has spent 4–7 years pursuing a Ph.D. or some other advanced degree. Instead, place your certifications or degrees in a section titled* Education and Certifications. *A master's degree might be the exception to this rule.*

Moran also discusses good strategies for breaking into the IT industry once you have earned your CCNA:

> *The most important factor is that you are moving toward a career goal. You might not get the title or job you want right out of school. If you can master those skills at your current position, while simultaneously building your network of contacts that lead to your dream position, you should be satisfied. You must build your career piece by piece. It won't happen all at once.*

Moran also outlines in his book that certifications such as the CCNA are part of an overall professional skill-set that you must continually enhance in order to further your IT career.

Your CCNA certificate proves that you are disciplined enough to commit to a rigorous course of study and follow through with your professional goals. It is unlikely that you will be hired simply because you have a CCNA, but it will place you ahead of other candidates. Even though you have listed the CCNA on your resume, it is important to highlight your networking skills that pertain to the CCNA in your job and skills descriptions on your resume.

Examining Certification Options

Although passing the CCNA exam is not an easy task, it is the starting point for more advanced Cisco certifications. When you log in to the online certification tracking tool (use the exam report to do this), be sure to view the certification progress link. This link provides specific information about professional-level certifications that you can work toward with your CCNA as the base.

Two common professional certifications are the Cisco Certified Network Professional (CCNP) and the Cisco Certified Security Professional (CCSP). Both of these certifications require you to pass multiple tests, but with a CCNA under your belt, continued network study and testing should feel more familiar.

If You Failed the Exam

If you fail your first attempt at the CCNA, you have to wait at least five calendar days after the day of the exam to retest. Stay motivated and sign up to take the exam again within a 30-day period of your first attempt. The score report outlines your weaknesses, and finding a study group or online community can help you with those difficult topics.

If you are familiar with the general concepts, focus on taking practice exams and memorizing the small details that make the exam so difficult. As a Cisco Networking Academy alumnus, you have access to the curriculum, and Packet Tracer provides an excellent simulator for most CCNA configurations. Consider your first attempt as a formal practice exam and as excellent preparation for passing the second attempt.

Summary

Whether you display your certificate and update your resume or prepare to conquer the test on your second attempt, remember to marvel at the innovation and creativity behind each concept you learn. The ability of our society to continually improve communication will keep you learning, discovering, and employed for a lifetime.

Your Notes

Index

SYMBOLS

A

X - Y - Z